50 Products:
Innovations in Design and Materials

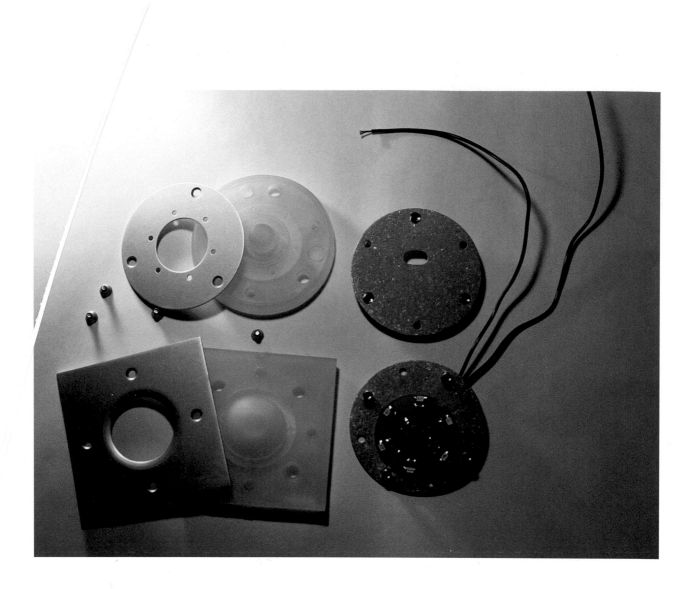

50 PRODUCTS

Innovations in Design and Materials

Mel Byars

Introduction by
David Revere McFadden

Research by
Cinzia Anguissola d'Altoé
Brice d'Antras

Technical drawings by
Marvin Klein

A Rotovision Book

PRO DESIGN SERIES

RotoVision

RotoVision

Published by RotoVision SA
Rue du Bugnon, 7
CH-1299 Crans-Près-Céligny
Switzerland

RotoVision SA
Sales & Production Office
Sheridan House
112/116A Western Road
Hove, East Sussex, BN3 IDD, England
Tel: +44 (0)1273 727268
Fax: +44 (0)1273 727269
e-mail: sales@RotoVision.com

Distributed to the trade in the United States
Watson-Guptill Publications
1515 Broadway
New York, NY 10036
U.S.A.

10 9 8 7 6 5 4 3 2

05 04 03 02 01 00 99 98

ISBN 2-88046-376-9

This book was written, designed, and
produced by Mel Byars

Printed in Singapore
Production and separation
by ProVision Pte Ltd, Singapore
Tel: +65 334 7720
Fax: +65 334 7721

PRO DESIGN SERIES

50 Chairs: Innovations in Design and Materials
by Mel Byars with an Introduction by Alexander von Vegesack

50 Tables: Innovations in Design and Materials
by Mel Byars with an Introduction by Sylvain Dubuisson

50 Lights: Innovations in Design and Materials
by Mel Byars with an Introduction by Paola Antonelli

50 Products: Innovations in Design and Materials
by Mel Byars with an Introduction by David Revere McFadden

50 Sports Wares: Innovations in Design and Materials
by Mel Byars with an Introduction by Florian Hufnagl

Contents

Introduction

The Body of Evidence:
Product Design at the Millennium

For most of the 20th century, art, craft, and design have formed an isosceles triangle, with art confidently located at the apex. Supporting this hierarchy of implicit values were systems of economics, politics, culture, and technology. While art has been at the tip of this creative iceberg for most of the past 100 years, the closing years of the century and the millennium suggest that the merging worlds of craft and design have the potential of toppling the cultural pyramid.

If there is one theme that informs creative activity as we approach the year 2000, it is a new and often surprising porosity among fields that have traditionally kept their distance from each other. Today, craft, design, architecture, fashion, and art have interpenetrated to a point where distinctions and definitions are useless, meaningless, or deceptive. This point is argued with passion and perception in the designs of Mel Byars's *50 Products* that range from conscientiously handcrafted objects and prototypes to mass-produced tools, containers, and gadgets intended from their creation to be, for the most part, cheap, plentiful, and accessible to all. Linking all of these designs, however, is an engagement with materials and process that brings the world of the crafts practitioner into the backyard of the industrial designer. These are all objects created and crafted with the user in mind. In their practicality, their intelligence, and their whimsy, they are profoundly humanistic.

Design is a mode of perception but also of action. Design helps us to see the world, to analyze needs, and to propose solutions. These objects of desire become metaphors for ourselves, our values, and our own bodies. The array of designs selected and highlighted by Mel Byars in *50 Products* are all ways of extending the actual and symbolic reach of our grasp. With these tools for the theater of daily life, we gather refuse, display our trophies, and eliminate pests. These products are the clear and poignant evidence of our bodies.

In a century marked by a radical technological progress

and innovation, medical advances and traumas, and spiritual quests and crises, our corporeal bodies have taken on new meaning. By using our senses of touch, sight, taste, hearing, and smell we are better equipped to confront and embrace the inevitable world of virtual, digital, and psychological realities. This understanding is not new. As early as 1856, the American philosopher, Ralph Waldo Emerson, noted, "Man is a shrewd inventor and is ever taking the hint of a new machine from his own structure, adapting some secret of his own anatomy in iron, wood, and leather, to some required function in the work of the world." It is the recognition of the fact that we are what we create, use, and treasure that underlines the real value of these designs. They are windows into our souls but windows firmly installed in the architecture of our bodies.

The 50 designs included in this volume, selected with uncanny insight and Byars's distinctively quirky point of view, are bellwethers for the changing climate of our times. They reveal the impressive knowledge brought to the design process by mature creators from around the world. They also give us intriguing clues about what may be over the near horizon and in the minds and understanding of emerging talent, those individuals described by the novelist, Henry Miller, as "the coming ones, the ones who are already scratching on the windowpanes."

This volume is truly a body of evidence of change, of the reinstatement of humanistic values, and of the growing porosity among disciplines that may be the most significant aspect of millennial culture.

David Revere McFadden
American Craft Museum
New York

Foreword:
A Loaf of Bread, a Jug of Wine, Thou,
and a Few Other Things

We love to talk about, to read about our stuff, possessions, objects, things, whatever you wish to call them. Certainly, normal everyday things have recently been the subject of numerous American books ranging from Donald A. Norman's *The Design of Everyday Things* and *The Psychology of Everyday Things* to Henry Petroski's *The Evolution of Useful Things* and even Susan Goldman Rubin's *Toilets, Toasters and Telephones: The How and Why of Everyday Objects*. And, of course, there is *The Origin of Things*, the 1947 work by German immigrant Julius E. Lips that reaches far back to the origins of our fetishistic past.

We embrace our possessions, things that might reveal our sophistication, social status, education, or a plethora of other personal criteria that we hope will distinguish us from others, make us different, possibly better. We have come to think that we direly need the objects of everyday life.

Children hold their possessions so dearly that most of them must be taught, or forced, to share them with others, particularly peers. In some places, have-not children in ghettos subjugate or kill other children to steal their expensive leather jackets or sports shoes, because these poor souls have been made to believe that they are what they wear, and, when they wear special clothing, they are somehow made to be special.

Rarely do we find someone so complete he asks only for "a loaf of bread, a jug of wine, and thou."

The world of domestic objects has become so diverse and crassly commercial and the subliminal forces of advertising machinery so effective that we sincerely feel that there are products without which we cannot function. And, of course, this is not true. For example, no one needs many of the domestic electrical appliances found in the home today, such as coffee makers, can openers, microwave ovens, pencil sharpeners, digital television sets, shoe and tooth brushes, knives, and an almost infinite number of other expensive, energy-sucking devices that are difficult to dispose of when we fall out of love with them shortly after we have married them.

Therefore, be not surprised when informed that this book does not suggest that you purchase or that you need any of the products here. However, these objects—ranging from the waggish and winsome to the serious and sublime—may indeed act like puppies in a kennel window who beg, "Take me home," in an unspoken language. Some of the items are indeed quite fetching.

Having been conjured by imaginative, adept designers during the last decade, these products are new. They express new ideas or offer innovative twists on old themes. For example, you will find a pop-up waste bin that is made of the kind of fabric and plastic used to produce tents (pages 138–139), a device that manages the tangle of cords cascading from our apparatus-hewn desks (pages 46–49), a low-tech insect killer that has been reinterpreted (pages 18–19), a teapot of ceramic that has the appearance of plastic (pages 66–69), flatware developed for McDonald's that disintegrates in little over a month (page 80–81), and much more to reveal that the breadth of problem solving and novelty can be engaging.

In the sometimes daunting task of gathering information and images, I was assisted by Cinzia Anguissola d'Altoé and Brice d'Antras, accomplished design scholars and teachers in their own right. This book and I have benefited greatly by their contributions. They, like sleuths in a British mystery novel, indefatigably and doggedly sought out the material, not only of my specific requests but of their own suggestions.

In the process of choosing the final entries for this book, certain important contextual aspects appeared. One circumstance that became clear is that the Dutch are particularly adept at creating the kind of objects this book concerns: ones that are small, non-electrical, non-battery operated, and domestic. Therefore, there may be an imbalance with the work from other countries, which there may very well be, and a prejudice shown, which there certainly was not. Another area of contention may be in the inclusion of two examples, rather than one example, of the work of Sebastian Bergne, a particularly distinguished

Foreword

Dutch, that this book considers.

Another aspect of this book may validate Mr. McFadden's observation in the Introduction about my "distinctively quirky point of view": When the final entries were chosen, which I did alone, I discovered that there was an inordinate number of vases. Rather than eliminate them or decrease the number, I decided to use the situation as an opportunity. Therefore, you will see how a diverse group of designers with different schooling, working for different manufacturers, under different circumstances, approach the same assignment—in this case, a vase—an object with more or less the same prerequisites that each designer must assume in solving the problem.

The circumstances surrounding the design of a vase as a paradigmatic object, as you can see here, vary greatly. One of the stories comes from Johan Bakermans, who in 1992, when a student at the polytechnical institution in The Hague, was asked to choose one project from a list of eleven suggested; his choice was "an adjustable vase." Bakermans told me, "Even though people have 101 vases, it's still possible to come home with a bouquet for which they don't have the right one. That's why I decided to do this project: to design a vase that you can adjust to the bouquet, instead of the other way around. I like to turn things upside down, to approach a product in a different way. This is how one can come up with a new product, a new function. That's why I decided to do this project." (See pages 104–107.)

Another example is a vase by Martin Brühl, who designs and makes art furniture sold through a small network of galleries in Holland. The owners of one of these galleries, One to Z in Delft and Rotterdam, suggested a certain vase design that would be suitable to both Brühl's aesthetic approach and his being the maker. The vase proved very successful, but, because the gallery was not capable of distributing it, Ed Mathon of The Edge/Sample from Industry included it in his firm's collection. Therefore, as Mathon has observed, "The idea for making this vase was triggered by salespeople." (See pages 108–109.)

Mathon also had another insight that had eluded me: "Holland is the country where the most flowers in the world are grown—no need to explain why every designer in The Netherlands comes up with the idea of making vases!"

All of this information proves that there is always more involved in the design of an object than meets the eye. There are probably long stories to be written about every object, even bad objects. And the examples here testify to the dedication of a whole new generation of designers and manufacturers who know that the production of good design can no longer be solely about shape and color. Good design must now include concerns for ecology, ergonomics, economics, politics, sociology, anthropology, and a range of other significant human factors. But let us not forget the converse: objects can and will be made that are merely entertaining and quite fatuous, diversions in a world where we may need relief or something silly to turn our attention from dire and depressing mishaps, our own or others which we see everyday on television.

Like the other volumes in RotoVision's Pro-Design Series about chairs, tables, and lighting, this volume includes the work of designers and manufacturers the world over, including those who work for manufacturers or editors on a freelance basis as well as others who are manufacturers' full-time employees. Yet, there is a new crop of entrepreneur-designers who serve as both creator and producer. This latter group is revolting against having to work for unenlightened, cloddish manufacturers in their own part of the world and feeling forced to immigrate to another country where they might be more appreciated. Now, by expanding the boundaries of possibility and by handling the manufacture of their own goods, they can stay in their own country, become productive, maybe even be happy.

Mel Byars
New York City

General Household Goods

Mail slot and catcher

Designers: WAAC's Design & Consultancy—
Joost Alferink (Dutch, b. 1964) and Dienand
Christie (Dutch, b. 1963)
Manufacturer: Gezu Borstel B.V., Nijkerk,
The Netherlands
Date of design: 1994–95

Produced by a longstanding brush manufacturer, this system is a transformation of the
formerly unimaginative plastic letter-slot fascia
into a stylish draft-resistant solution available
in a range of colors. An inexpensive post-
catcher envelope prevents mail from spilling
onto the floor.

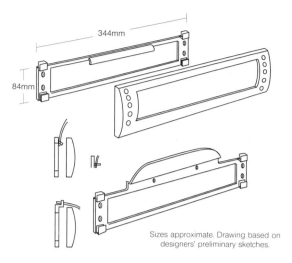

Sizes approximate. Drawing based on
designers' preliminary sketches.

Like baleen in a whale's
mouth, a dense row of
plastic whiskers wards
off cold drafts entering
through the shoot.

Outside fascia (facing
hallway or out of doors)
in injection-molded transparent ABS (acrylonitrile-
butadiene-styrene) in a
range of transparent
and printed colors.

Details of mail-
catch pouch and
ABS holding lever.

In their drawings, notice
one of many of the
designers' attempts to
solve the baleen-like
draft-resistant design.

Laser-cut polypropylene mail
pouch is removable at the top
with an easy-to-release ABS lever.

"Spore" doorbell buttons

Designers: Tom Gordon (American, b. 1966)
and Ted Pierson (American, b. 1967)
Manufacturer: the designers' firm, spOre Inc.,
Seattle, WA, U.S.A.
Date of design: 1995

This attractive, soundly engineered door
button features a long-life LED light source
that lasts over 11 years and consumes only
one watt of electricity. The idea behind the
design is, of course, for the door signal
button to be seen out of doors at night. A
comparison of the warm, soft button in the
round version to a human nipple may be
unavoidable.

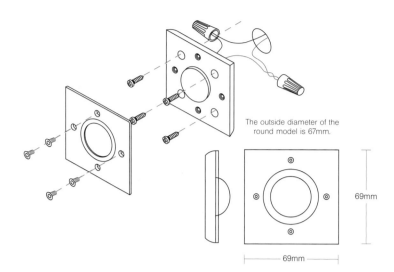

The outside diameter of the round model is 67mm.

69mm

69mm

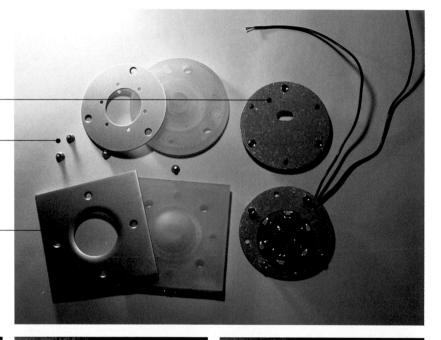

5052 aluminum back plate cut with computerized punch, tumble deburred, 4-40 threaded Standoffs pressed on, and screened with graphics.

Stainless-steel screws (attached with wire nuts).

5052 aluminum face plate is cut with a computerized punch; the milled surface is finished, etched, and anodized (attached with stainless-steel screws).

Warm (from the light source) and soft-to-the-touch button in green or amber injection-molded Dynaflex elastomer with UV (ultra-violet) additive.

"Machine" humidifier

Designers: Bruno Gregori (Italian, b. 1954) and
Setsu Ito (Japanese, b. 1964)
Manufacturer: Il Coccio Umidificatori, Barberino
del Mugello (FI), Italy
Date of design: ca. 1996

Called an "artificial organ" by its designers
and having the appearance of a miniature
ocean liner, this humidifier, made of hard,
heat-resistant pottery, is placed on a radiator
after being filled with water. With only a single
small opening, cleaning may be difficult. The
manufacturer has been producing a variety
of humidifiers for over 35 years.

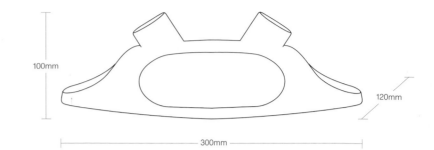

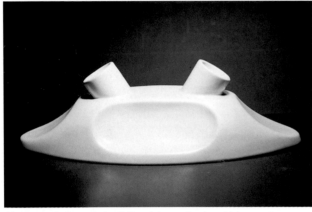

The ceramic formula for Il Coccio's production originates from
experimentation in the research department of chemistry in
Florence, Italy. The material is a combination of argil (potter's
clay) and kaolin (clay filler or extender) with a high evaporation
capacity, strained in chalk molds.

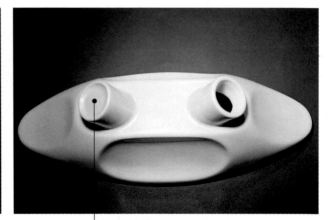

Probably for symmetry's sake, this vessel
features two chimney-like extensions, but
only one is open, facilitating the vessel's
being filled with water and permitting the
eventual escape of steam.

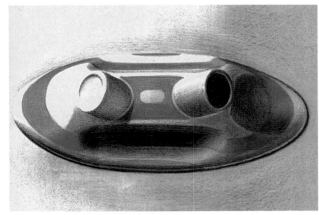

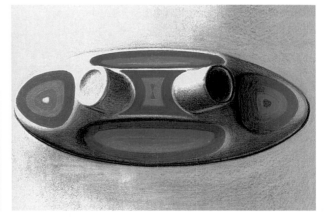

One of 21 pieces in the firm's "Il Coccio d'Autore" range by mostly
Italian designers, this piece was originally considered for decora-
tion (above and right). Fortunately, it was left white.

"Dr. Skud" fly swatter

Designer: Philippe Starck (French, b. 1949)
Manufacturer: Alessi S.p.A., Crusinallo (VB), Italy
Date of design: 1998

Despite its proportions, this object is very sturdy.
Its rigidity was made possible by forming a single,
non-composite material thick in some areas (the
stem and base) and thin in another (the paddle).
The most distinguishing feature of this somewhat
insignificant object is of course the Fornasetti face
in the paddle; the image is made possible
by various sizes of little round openings, the same
dot process that makes images in black-and-
white halftone printing. This delightful product
may entice people to own it whether they have
flies or not.

93mm

440mm

67mm

The injection-molded
thermoplastic paddle
section, where the face is
formed by a pierced-dot
pattern, is formed in the
thin area of the mold so
that significant malleability
is possible.

The stem and base are
formed thicker in the mold
than the paddle to create
the rigidity required for the
object to be self-standing
on the floor.

As often happens in
the original stages of a
concept, the manufacturer
realized that the base
had to be made wider
for balance.

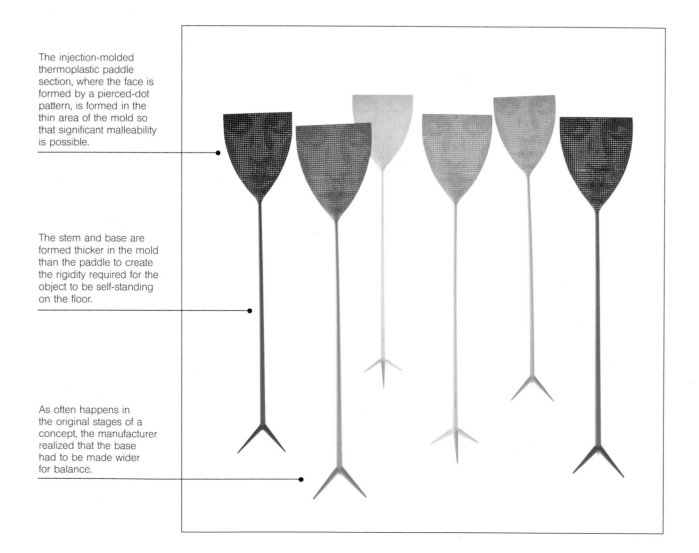

"Daisy" door mat

Designer: Jeffrey Bernett (American, b. 1964)
Manufacturer: 1997–98 by the designer; from
1998 by Asplund, Stockholm, Sweden
Date of design: 1997

With the intension of adding humor or a light-
heartedness to a domestic décor, the designer
used a standard material (cocoa matting) but
in an interesting shape, rather than a plain
rectangular one. He created an object that solves
the problem of what he describes as "hallways
that are uneventful and really quite boring"
in apartment buildings with monotonous
rows of front doors. The mat is also made in
other shapes.

761mm
diameter

A crafts knife was used to cut out the daisy shape from
the matting material. In the later production process, the
shape is stamped out with a die by hydraulic machinery.

For his early handmade versions, the
designer traced a pink paper pattern on
the backside of the coir matting (cocoa
matting with a rubber backing).

In the handmade version,
a completed door mat lies
beside its negative trim.

"Microservizi domestici" ("Microservice" holder)

Designer: Massimo Varetto (Italian, b. 1963)
Manufacturer: Opos, Milano, Italy
Date of design: 1996

This designer declares that he likes bolts, screws, threaded bars, and structural aluminum with rivets, springs, and the like rather than nails, glue, and welding because the latter do not allow for control and flexibility. Known for his highly unorthodox, whimsical approach, he claims, "I find that I am like a dog trying to bite his tail. I discard the nail in favor of the bolt. . . . I am moved by anonymous and humble objects that I find at one instant and then can't find anymore."

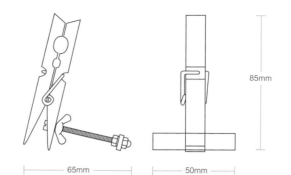

The seven elements of this object include a wing nut, two octagonal nuts, a washer, an aluminum brace bar, a threaded bolt, and a standard wooden clothes pin. (Of course, the clothes pin itself is composed of three pieces, but it was acquired in tact from a manufacturer.)

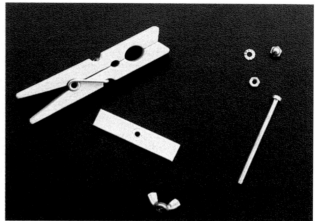

The thought, planning, and effort that went into the packaging may reveal that this product has been taken with far more seriousness by its designer and producer that one might suspect.

In illustrating how his object works, the designer reveals the lightheardedness infused in all his work.

Christmas-tree ornament

Designers: Andreas Brandolini (German, b. 1951)
Manufacturer: anthologie quartett, Bad Essen, Germany
Date of design: 1993

Based on the silhouette of a typical German Christmas
tree, this hand-painted glass ornament was mouth
blown to the designer's specifications at the Krebs Glas
Lauscha GmbH in Rosenheim, Germany, the place
where the first Christmas-tree ornaments were made
150 years ago. The firm, anthologie quartett, chose to
celebrate its tenth anniversary by commissioning objects
of "almost totally no practical use" but made according
to the traditional techniques used by the renowned
glass makers of the Thuringian forest. An ornament by
Wilhelm Wagenfeld (1900–90) of 1930–31 was also
included in the group.

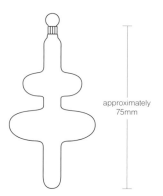

approximately
75mm

A glass maker mouth blows an object according to ancient
techniques at the Lauscha glass factory where Christmas
tree ornaments, like the ones shown here, have been made
for over one-and-a-half centuries.

The inside of an ornament is coated with mercury
after the form is completed, thus creating a shimmer-
ing effect. The outside is painted with colors on the
super-thin glass surface.

By Ginbande-Design

By Alessandro Mendini

By Nelly Putzer

By C. Giunnelli and M. Panza

8

"Cocktail" object-holder curtain

Designer: Olivier Peyricot (French, b. 1969)
Manufacturer: Axis, Villejuif, France
Date of design: 1995

Not much different from a shower-curtain liner, this product is a clever concept. Strips of sanded PVC are welded by high-frequency machinery to the overall sheet, thus forming 126 square pockets into which anything flat or thin can be inserted. The curtain can be hung against a wall or used as a room divider.

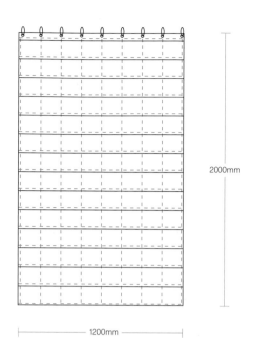

2000mm

1200mm

14 strips of sanded PVC (polyvinylchloride) are placed horizontally across a single sheet and high-frequency heat sealed forming pockets. (See the vertical lines.)

The doubled-over top edge is high-frequency heat sealed. The holes through which plastic hoops are inserted are also heat sealed.

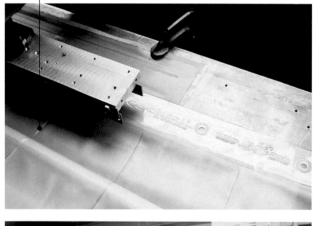

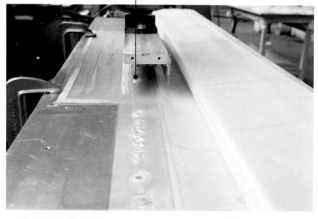

An operator works at a high-frequency welding machine used to make this product.

A close view of the top edge shows the curtain hanging from plastic shower-curtain hoops. Various items—including stamps, photographs, a CD, and a watch—can be housed in the pockets.

"The Switch"

Designer: Radi—Claudio Colucci
(Italian, b. 1965), Florence Doléac Stadler
(French, b. 1968), Laurent Massaloux
(French, b. 1968), Olivier Sidet (French,
b. 1965), and Robert Stadler (Austrian,
b. 1966)
Manufacturer: prototype
Date of design: 1995

A highly sophisticated version of an
on-off electrical switch, this mechanism
is far more ingenious than it may appear.
When bent, the flow of electrical current
is stopped, and, when straightened, the
contact is remade.

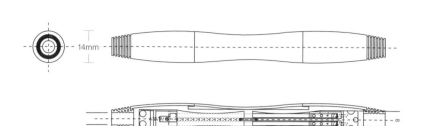

As these photographs clearly illustrate, when the switch section of
the cord is straight (left) the electrical current flows through the
wires, and, when bent (right), the connection is broken.

"The Switch"

These dual metaphors of a cord and a straw reveal the bare basics of how "The Switch" works.

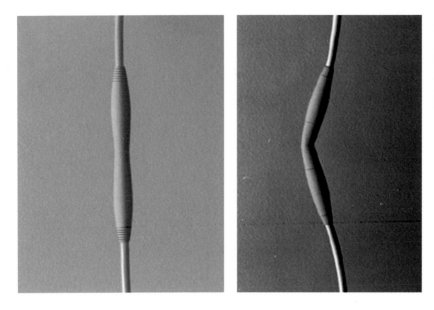

Electrical current flows when the switch section is straight (left), but is interrupted when bent (right). As part of a normal electrical-cord extension, this thin and unobtrusive switch has the appearance of a very thin snake that may have swallowed a larger snake.

Computer-generated technical drawings of the injection-molded thermoplastic polyurethane outer housing in the form of a double ellipse (above) and the compression-molded polyepoxy structure of the bending mechanism inside (below).

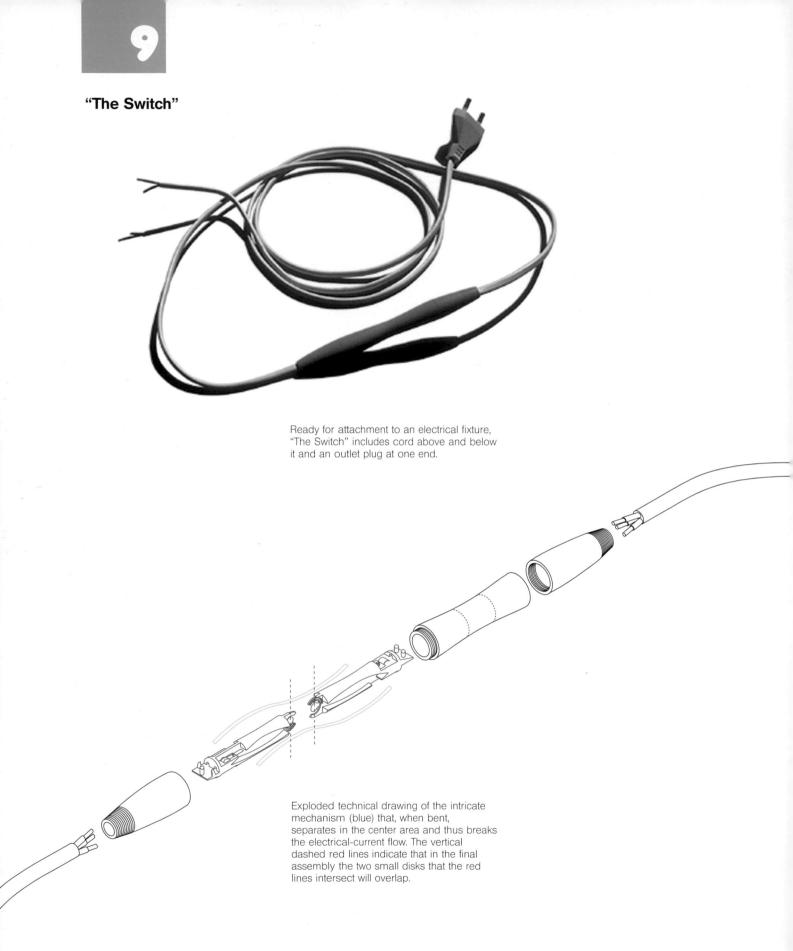

9

"The Switch"

Ready for attachment to an electrical fixture, "The Switch" includes cord above and below it and an outlet plug at one end.

Exploded technical drawing of the intricate mechanism (blue) that, when bent, separates in the center area and thus breaks the electrical-current flow. The vertical dashed red lines indicate that in the final assembly the two small disks that the red lines intersect will overlap.

Office Accouterments

"CUTFISH" scissors

Designer: Francesco Filippi (Italian, b. 1956)
Manufacturer: Kreo S.r.l., Milano, Italy
Date of design: 1990

Accepting the challenge to produce a whole, new, different concept in scissor design, this designer also chose to incorporate the images of a cat and a fish as a playful gesture distinct from function. These scissors, like standard ones, are composed of two parts hinged together. This version can be used by right- or left-handed people. There may be some question as to the cutting efficiency of the product. (For a letter opener formed from a section of a pair of standard scissors, see pages 44–45.)

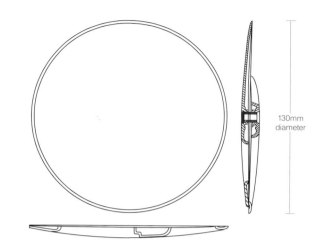

130mm diameter

Right- or left-hand usage is possible.

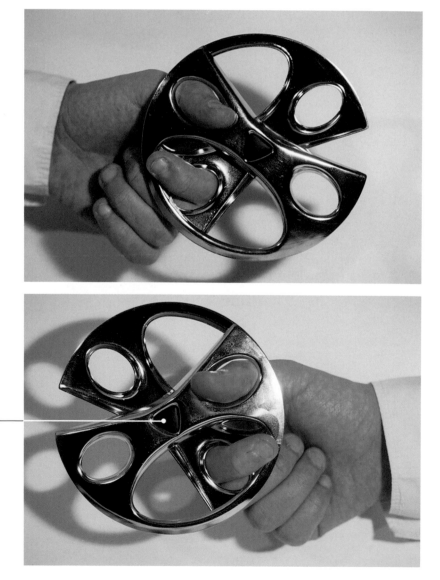

Triangular-headed male and female bolts and a plastic washer hold together each of the two rotating parts.

"CUTFISH" scissors

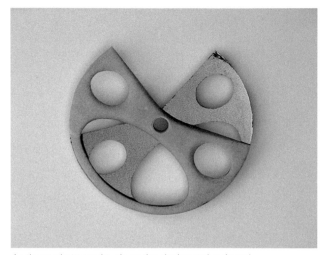

As these photographs show, the designer developed many prototypes, shown here in sequence. The polypropylene prototype is above.

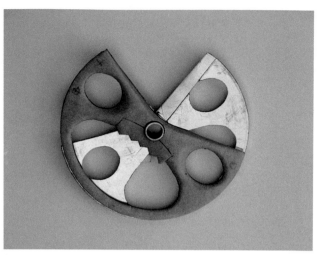

Polypropylene and tin prototype.

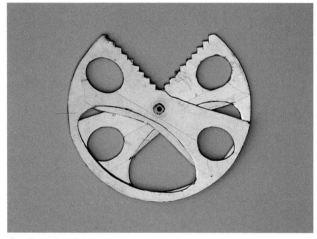

Cardboard prototype.

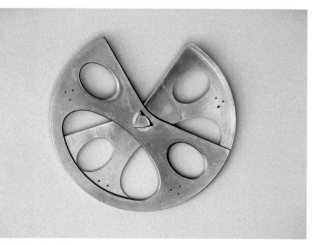

Working aluminum prototype.

The circular elements are hydraulically stamped out. They are shown here open (below) and closed (above). The metal is stainless steel coated with titanium by PVD (physically vaporized deposition) to create a highly resistant surface that is in turn electrolytically polished.

The packaging.

"Curva" ruler

Designers: De Denktank—Patrick Kruithof
(Dutch, b. 1968) and Eelco Rietveld
(Dutch, b. 1969)
Manufacturer: The Edge/Sample from
Industry, Rotterdam, The Netherlands
Date of design: 1995

Imaginatively drawing upon the use of
refuse material that is normally discarded
by manufacturers, this design team put
old aluminum venetian-blind slats to good
use as rulers. With its ideal curve making
it easy to pick up and move, black-ink
graphics are silkscreen printed onto the
pre-existing base colors of old slats.

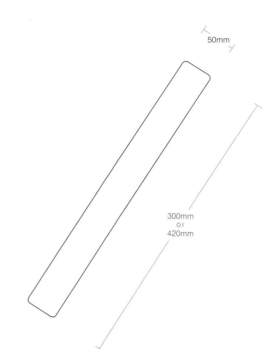

The producer of this ruler recycles 50mm-wide
venetian blind slats (a standard in the industry)
that have been either already used as blinds
(post-consumer waste) or discarded as refuse
(pre-consumer waste) by one or another major
manufacturer. Here it is shown as a window-
covering assembly complete with card and pull.

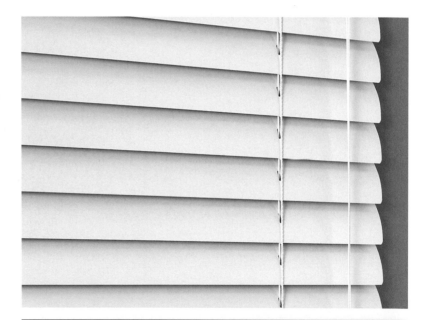

Graphics are silkscreen printed on 50mm-wide
venetian-blind slats that have already been
spray painted in a range of colors by a manufacturer of blinds; a modification in the printing has
to be made for the convex shape. The corners
are round-cut like standard venetian blind slats.

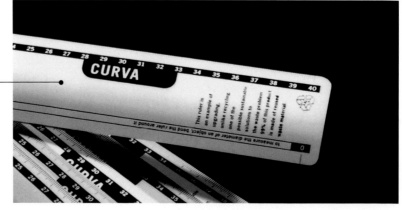

"Artergo 1" writing pens

Designer: Takahiro Okamoto (Japanese, b. 1948)
Manufacturer: the designer's firm, Eyetopia,
Osaka, Japan
Date of design: 1996

This designer as manufacturer in his myriad experimentations made prototypes of writing pens in a vast number of shapes and sizes in an attempt to satisfy all, or possibly almost all, of the different human hand types as well as peculiar grasping methods. He eventually settled on two models; each employs different molding methods.

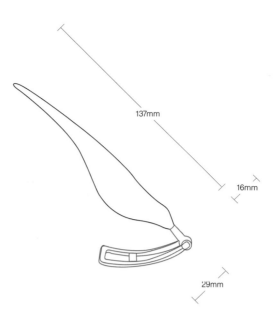

The "Artergo 1" pen (right) is injection-molded ABS (acrylonitrile-butadiene-styrene), painted blue or tan. A metal mold is used.

The number of possible shapes and sizes are obviously limited only by the imagination. These experimental models were made of clay and painted.

Reflecting the ergonomic hand-conforming concept of the "Artergo 1," these "Ergo-Boys" are formed in inexpensive rubber molds. Available only in blue, the pen shapes are all different, but the bases are the same.

Document clip

Designer: Bernard Moïse (French, b. 1966)
Manufacturer: Les Éditions Ardi, Mere-Montfort l'Amaury, France
Date of design: 1990 (first version), 1994 (second version)

Based on an invention of many years ago, this wall-mounted note-and-document holder was first developed by this designer as a three-part system and was finally refined as a simple mechanism composed of a single aluminum section that holds a heavy metal ball. The foundry that makes this object specializes in aluminum fabrication.

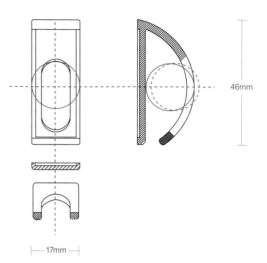

46mm

17mm

Early drawings by the designer reveal his early pursuit of abstracted biomorphic shapes.

The first version is composed of the cage, ball, and wire fence.

The cage is polished cast aluminum (poured by gravity).

The ball is solid tempered steel.

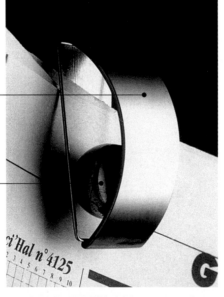

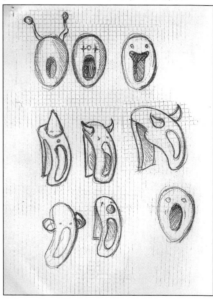

The second version is composed of a pierced cage and a ball only.

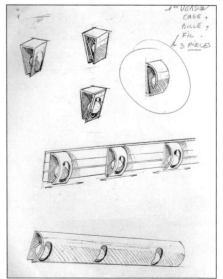

At one point, the designer explored the possibility of a tandem arrangement.

"Scissors" letter opener

Designer: Peter van der Jagt (Dutch, b. 1971)
Manufacturer: The Edge/Sample from
Industry, Rotterdam, The Netherlands
Date of design: 1995

This metaphor was inspired by that fact that
some people use scissors to open mail. This
designer offers the solution of half of a pair
of standard-design scissors. But he and
the manufacturer had difficulties in getting
one side of a pair of scissors that was not
already sanded, polished, nickel plated, and,
most importantly, drilled in the center with
a hole. Fortunately they were able to find a
factory willing to disrupt their production
and produce half scissors in small numbers,
undrilled and unplated. (For an operational
pair of scissors, see pages 34–37.)

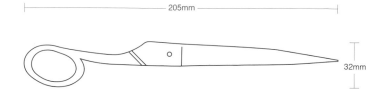

One side of a pair of
scissors is available either
silverplated in the standard
version or is available
chromium, gold, or nickel
plated. The letter opener
is shown here with its
package.

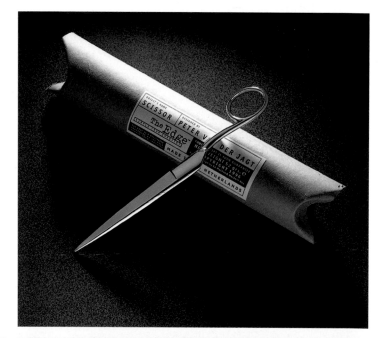

Below, in a factory in Solingen, Germany, the
renowned center for fine cutlery manufacture, a
large CNC (computer numeric controlled) pressure
machine molds scissor blades into rough versions
known in German as *Rohlings*. The computer control
panel is shown in the inset to the right.

The *Rohlings* are sharpened by hand before the plating occurs.

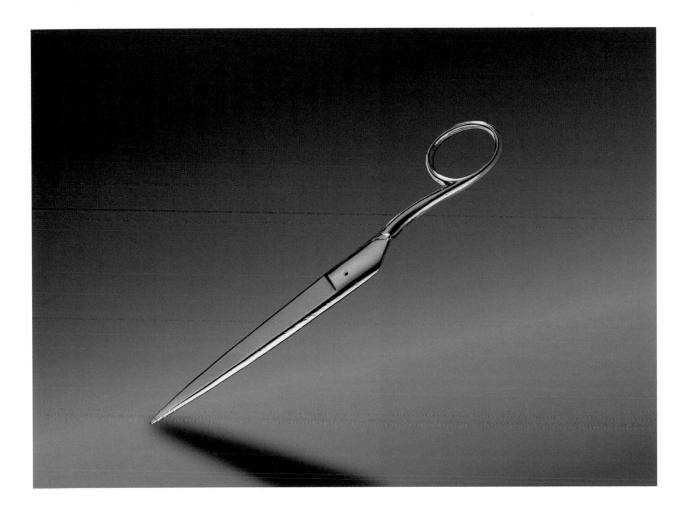

"Cable Turtle" cord manager

Designer: Flex Development B.V. (Dutch)
Manufacturer: Cleverline, Rotterdam, The Netherlands
Date of design: 1996

Available in a range of pastel or bright colors, this product was invented to help in eliminating the tangled mess of electronic cords cascading down from an array of appliances and equipment scattered across working surfaces. The Germany Gute Industrie Form prize committee cited the Cable Turtle as "an ingenious yet simple innovation," and it was granted a gold metal at the International Inventions Fair in Geneva, Switzerland. About 800,000 units were made in its first year of production, 1997.

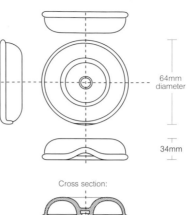

64mm diameter

34mm

Cross section:

An electrical outlet cord can be shortened to eliminate the tangle falling from one's desk. The cord here is being wound around the "Cable Turtle" before each end is folded inward.

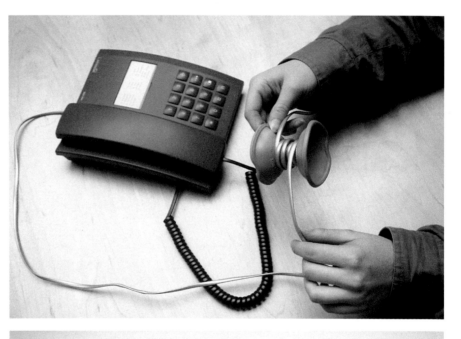

A developmental concept drawing.

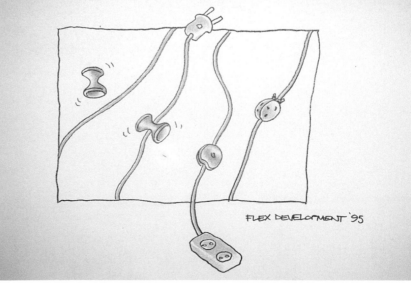

FLEX DEVELOPMENT '95

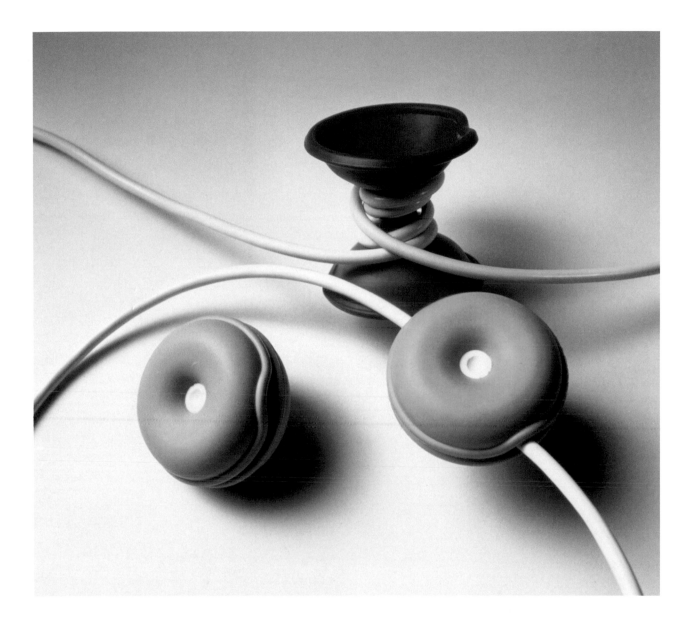

"Cable Turtle" cord manager

An injection machine is infusing a mold with SBR (a polyester-based thermoplastic elastomer).

The packaging was designed by Millford–Van den Berg Design.

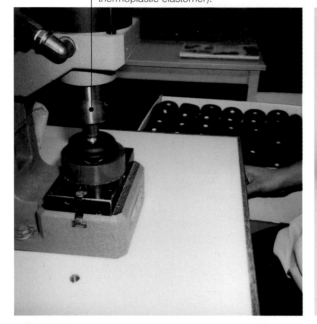

Since two identical sections comprise the objects, only a single mold is necessary. Each section is snap fitted, one to the other, by an axle.

Illustrations adapted from a drawing by Flex Development B.V.

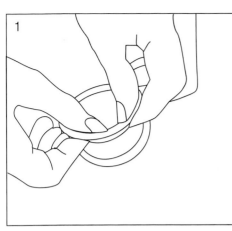

Each cup is folded outward.

The cord is wrapped around the center axle until the desired length of cord remains at each end section.

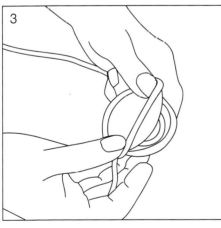

The cups are then folded inward again, enclosing the wrapped cord.

A lip on each side of each cup allows the cord's exit.

"Soft" object holder

Designers: Sỳn—Marina Paul (Italian, b. 1960)
and Francesco Scansetti (Italian, b. 1955)
Manufacturer: Outlook Zelco Europe S.r.l.,
Presezzo (BE), Italy
Date of design: 1996

That this object mirrors, intentionally or not, the human female sex organ is undeniable. And that it is used for the insertion of other objects may have been an unfortunate choice for the design metaphor. Nevertheless, calling on the elastic, flexible, and washable qualities of expanded polyurethane resin, the designers created a receptacle, whether placed horizontally or vertically, that can hold a wide range of objects. 10,000 units were made the first year of production, 1997.

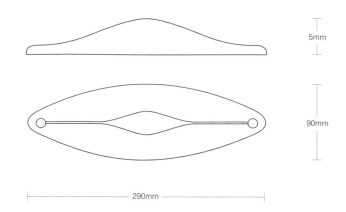

The receptacle has a wide range of functional possibilities. It may be screwed to a wall as well as placed on a flat surface.

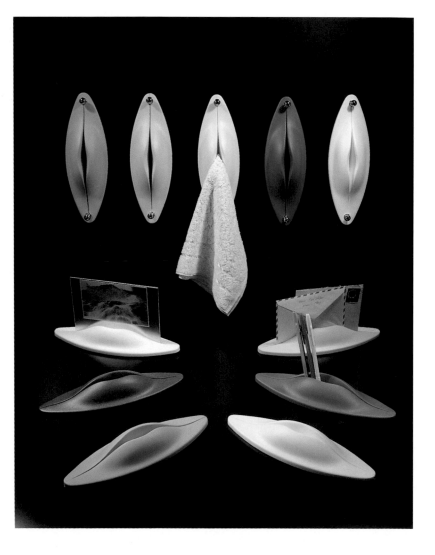

"Soft" object holder

Wooden prototype and early production models and trials.

The package and product were both designed by the same couple.

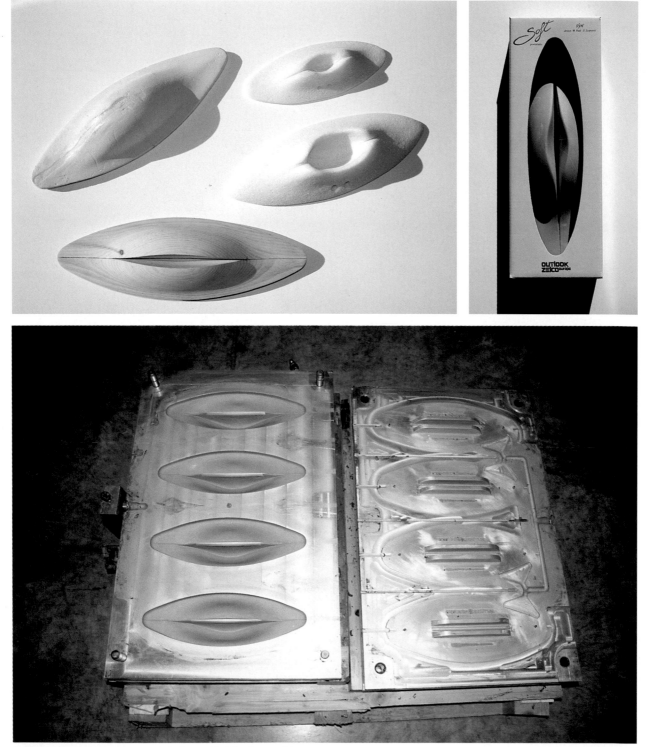

Soft expanded polyurethane resin is formed in injection molds.

Kitchen and Dining Wares

Trivet

Designers: Santina Bonini (Italian, b. 1961) and
Ernesto Spicciolato (Italian, b. 1957)
Manufacturer: Hopeful Rubber Manufacturing
Co. Ltd., Kowloon, Hong Kong, for Viceversa,
Florence, Italy
Date of design: 1995

Even though many products today may give the
impression that they are made with the use of
highly sophisticated machinery, most, like this
trivet, probably are not. Using little more than
a pair of dies in a compression machine, these
trivets are formed under high heat and finished
essentially by hand. The Italian designers had to
submit very precise drawings for the die making
and manufacture in the Far East.

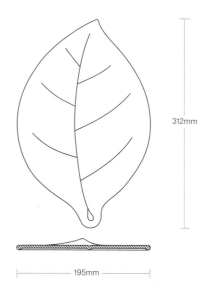

312mm

195mm

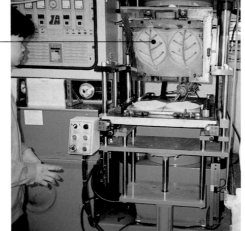

The tops of the pair
of molding dies, fitted
to a compression
molding machine.

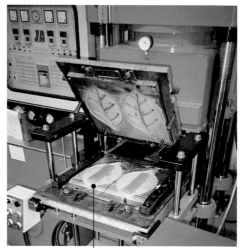

Slabs of HTV silicon rubber
are placed on the bottom
die, much like batter in a
waffle iron.

Keeping each trivet
warm after forming, a
workman trims off the
excess materials
around each object.

The finished trivets are able to tolerate high temp-
eratures up to 220°C to insulate and protect
kitchen work tops or dining table surfaces from
hot pots, irons, and such. The material is food-
grade approved and safe for food contact.

"Cricket" plastic-bottle compactor

Designer: Julian Brown (British, b. 1955)
Manufacturer: Rexite S.p.A., Cusago (MI), Italy
Date of design: 1997

A low-tech tool made with high-tech machinery,
this plastic-bottle compressor consists of essentially two main components: a two-part (top and
bottom) plastic device between which an empty
bottle is placed and steel tubes along which the
top plastic device slides downward. You use
your foot to press down on a captured empty
bottle, steadying yourself with the plastic knobs
at the top ends of each metal tube. By compact-
ing bottles, for example, your garbage bulk is
decreased.

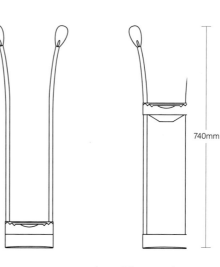

The handles of the device are
made of zinc-plated steel and the
crushing pallets and handle
knobs of polypropylene. A 200-
ton injection-molding machine is
seen in the background.

A prototype, based on CNC milling of
solid materials, was constructed in
ABS, steel, and silicone rubber.

On this prototype, a PET (polyethylene
terephthalate) bottle is posed for
crushing by a swift stamp of the foot.

"Mr. & Mrs. Prickly" salt and pepper shakers

Designer: Nick Crosbie (British, b. 1971)
Manufacturer: Inflate Ltd, London, England
Date of design: 1997

The design team and manufacturer, one and the same, began their business venture with the design and production of inflatable objects (see the book, *50 Lights: Innovations in Design and Materials*). The team members, including Nick Crosbie, have retained their interest in the use of soft and malleable plastics and turned their attention to products in PVC (polyvinylchloride).

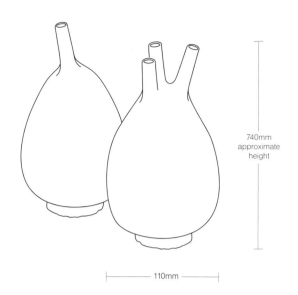

740mm approximate height

110mm

Employing a process like that for making rubber gloves, molds in ovoid shapes are dipped into liquefied PVC. The marking "INFLATE" on the sides of the mold sections were made by the mold maker.

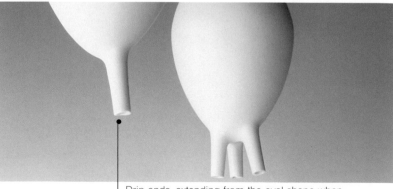

Drip ends, extending from the oval shape when removed from the liquid material, form different "stalactites" that are cut off at the ends to form the nipples out of which the salt or pepper is squirted.

"Tohot" salt and pepper shakers

Designer: Jean-Marie Massaud (French, b. 1966)
Manufacturer: Authentics of artipresent GmbH, Holtzgerlingen, Germany
Date of design: 1998

This product was produced in polypropylene, a translucent plastic material for which the manufacturer has become well known. Presumably one of the most notable features of the connective device—a magnet—is that one section remains attached to the other while stored, thus preventing separation of an inseparable couple.

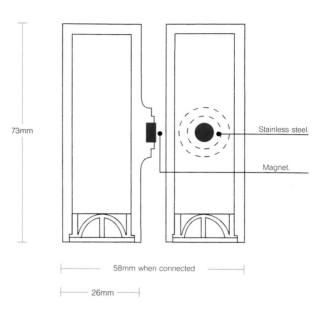

73mm

Stainless steel.

Magnet.

58mm when connected

26mm

The body of the shakers is injection-molded transparent polypropylene, highly appealing in light or pastel colors.

The units can be attached to each other via a magnet fused into the side of one unit and a stainless steel disk, to which the magnet adheres, in the other.

Decanter-and-drinking-glass set

Designer: Tord Boonji (Dutch, b. 1968) and
Emma Woffenden (British, b. 1962)
Manufacturer: the designers' firm, tranSglass,
London, Great Britain
Date of design: 1997

Acquiring the sponsorship of Perrier-Joüet, this
design couple reprocesses wine bottles that
they choose with great discernment, depending
on the ultimate purpose. For example, thin-
sided bottles are desirable as drinking glasses,
while thick-sided ones are more appropriate as
decanters. Possibly not revealed in the images
here, the tableware that these designers make
themselves has finesse and refinement.

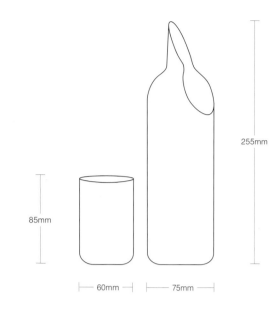

85mm

255mm

60mm   75mm

Based on color, form, and wall-thickness, wine bottles for
decanters as well as other tableware by these designers
are selected from a glass recycling plant in London. Not
all bottles are appropriate. For example, only those with
long necks are made into decanters. After selection, the
bottles are washed, and labels removed.

21

Decanter

A diamond-blade table saw is used to remove the bottle neck and reform the opening.

The bottle spout after the first cut is quite rough and needs finishing.

A water-fed diamond lap grinding wheel that is graduated from coarse mesh sizes to finer ones, smooths the surface of the spout. The water makes for a smoother surface and lowers the friction-created temperature. The brushes around the edge of the wheel prevent particles and water from flying outward.

After successive stages of grinding.

3

4

5

6

The edges are beveled and further polished with a felt disk and pumice.

The decanter is sandblasted, brush polished to remove the dryness and create a silky finish, cleaned, and fired at 570°C in a kiln for enamel transference of the logo.

22

Teapot

Designer: Ole Jensen (Danish, b. 1958)
Manufacturer: 1993–97 produced by Royal
Copenhagen A/S and sold by Paustian A/S,
both Copenhagen, Denmark; from 1997
produced and sold by Royal Copenhagen
Date of design: 1993

Due to the wide use of inexpensive but
expressive plastics today, you may guess, at
first sight, that this object is made of a slick-
surfaced synthetic material. Contrarily, the
substance is actually an ancient one—faience—
evidence that traditional materials are still
being successfully employed in the production
of everyday objects. The complicated nature of
its voluptuous form necessitated the designer's
developing the concept for a special four-
part mold.

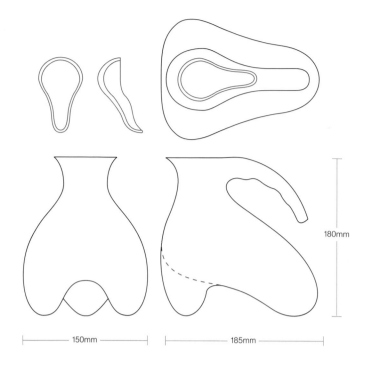

180mm

150mm   185mm

A loose spoon-like
lid is pressed down
to allow pouring.

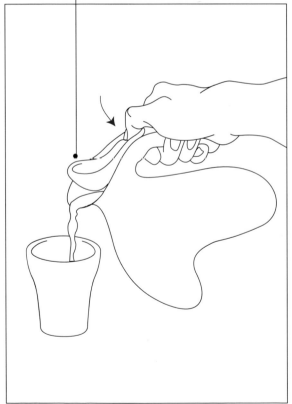

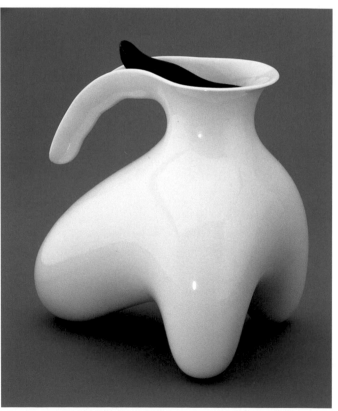

The colors of the body and the lid are contrasting offering a more
distinctive appearance than had they matched.

Teapot

Due to the extravagant proportions of the body, a four-part mold configuration was devised by the designer (shown here in his own drawing). (For a similar problem, see pages 128–131.)

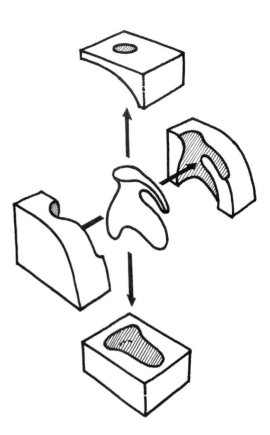

In the manufacturer's large production facility, slip (clay and water) is poured into open plaster molds for the body, but the lids are hand cast in closed plaster molds (not shown).

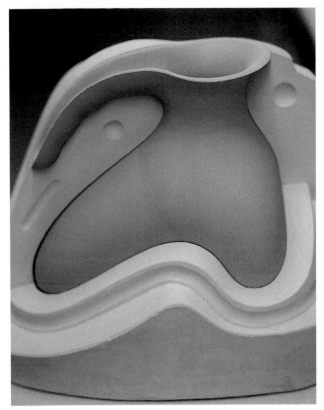

A fully formed teapot after the clay partially dries.

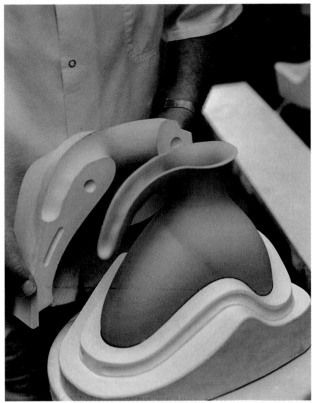

A workman removes one side of the four-part mold.

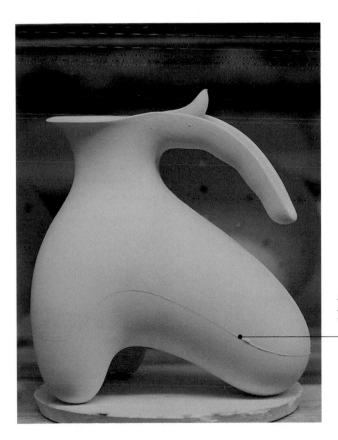

A teapot after casting and before the mold lines are abrased, the full faience glaze is applied, and firing occurs at 1200°C.

Teapots

Designers: Leona Matějková and
Gabriela Náhlíková (both Czech, b. 1966)
Manufacturer: Studio MM, Dalovice,
Czech Republic
Date of design: 1997

Like the furniture and furnishings that C.R.
Mackintosh designed for Miss Cranston's
Tearooms in Glasgow, so these designers
produced these teapots also for a tearoom.
The production is traditional; the inter-
changeable parts make them special.

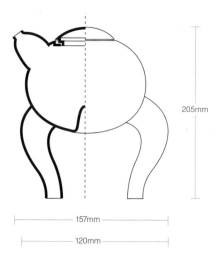

157mm

120mm

205mm

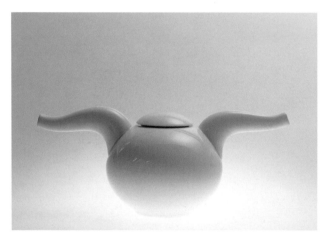

The handles, spouts, and legs are all of the same shape,
facilitating each pot's elements' being assembled in different
combinations—for example, the handle of one pot may also
serve as the spout of another.

Models for sectional mold making.

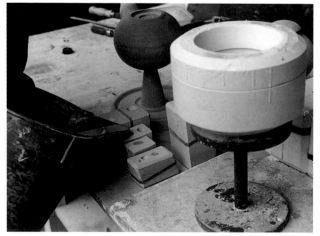

On a work table there is the plaster mold for the body in the
foreground, a wooden model of the body in the background,
and slip being poured into molds at left.

"Space Lily" fruit bowl

Designer: Christopher Procter (American,
b. 1958) and Fernando Rihl (Brazilian,
b. 1962)
Manufacturer: Spatial Interference Ltd,
London
Date of design: 1997

Rather than using one piece of acrylic
sheeting and bending it in several
places, these designers have chosen to
combine three sections, each bent in
three places to form a triangular base
with one section overlapping the other.
The tints of the acrylic planes, seen one
through the other, reflect vibrant hues.

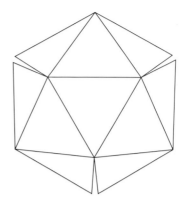

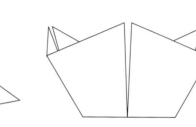

140mm

370mm

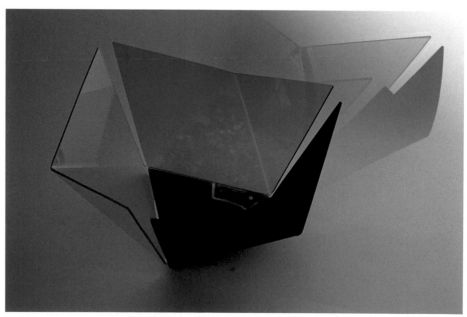

CNC (computer numeric controlled) machinery is employed for the cutting and
engraving to assure precise dimensions and fit. Three sections, or pedals, are
placed one on the other and screwed together for each bowl.

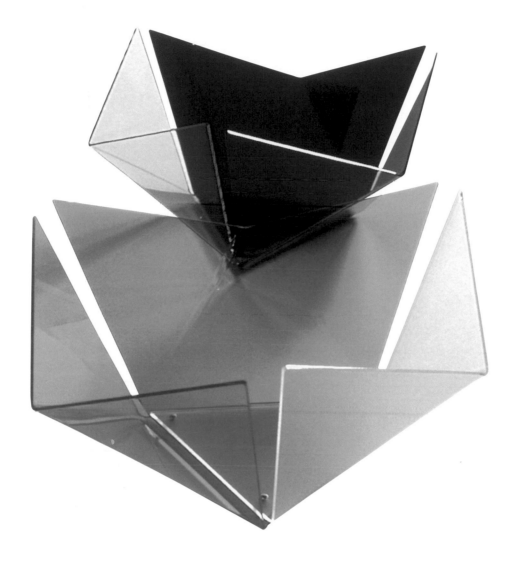

"Space Lily" fruit bowl

3mm acrylic sections in various colors (matt, tinted, and live edged) are CNC (computer numeric control) router cut and engraved.

The folds are made on a form with localized heat.

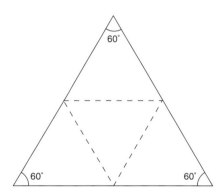

The geometrics of the configuration are based on a 60° angle.

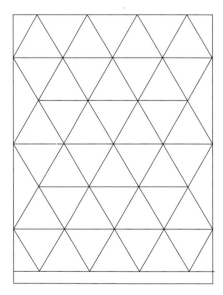

Stainless-steel bolts and nuts.

Three holes are bored into the triangular base of each of the three sections.

Edges are flame polished.

Three self-locking screws and bolts are counter sunk in the base, holding firm the three sections of a completed bowl.

"Flat" bowls

Designer: Marco Susani (Italian, b. 1956)
and Mario Trimarchi (Italian, b. 1958)
Manufacturer: Serafino Zani S.r.l., Lumezzane
Gazzolo (BR), Italy
Date of design: 1996

These bowls are part of a range of objects
named "Zero's," referring to the zeros or the
naughts of the first decade of the 21st century.
Very thin, transparent polypropylene shapes
are twisted into bowls by the end user.
Unlike origami, the shapes are not made by
creasing. The price of 10,000 L. ($6, £4,
18 F.) for one bowl is so cheap, one wonders
how the manufacturer makes the effort
worthwhile.

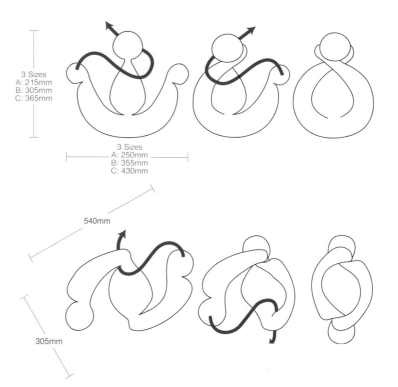

Steel prototypes were developed prior to production.

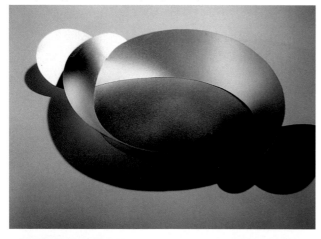

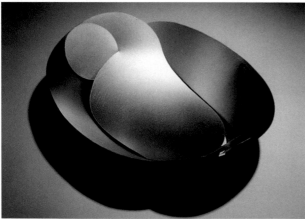

The yellow silhouette (top) is the flat stage of the folded red bowl
(bottom). Flat shapes are stamped out of polypropylene sheets
(1mm thick) and folded (or, as the manufacturer says, "knotted")
into bowls.

"Tube Basket"

Designer: Ross Tuthill Menuez (American, b. 1965)
Manufacturer: the designer's firm, Prototype and Production, Brooklyn, NY, U.S.A.
Date of design: 1996

This vessel differs from traditional Guatemalan all-purpose baskets only in the use of materials; the technique is the same. In this case, the weaving of the industrial tubing, on which the manufacturer's printing specifications are retained, is begun from a metal armature at the base.

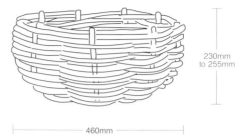

230mm to 255mm

460mm

Weaving is begun with a nine-pointed star of stainless-steel rods (9mm diameter).

The metal rods are fed into polyurethane tubing (9mm diameter, 6mm wall thickness) to form the base.

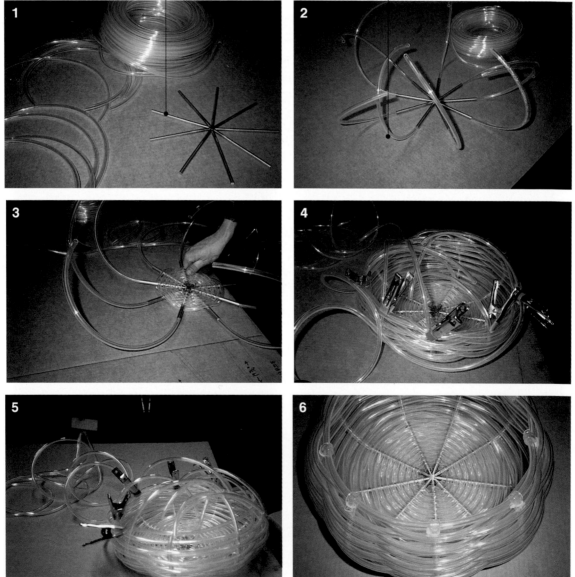

During the weaving, sections are held in place with pinch clamps.

A completed basket has been finished and secured with nylon cable ties.

"Mater-Bi" flatware

Designer: Antoni Zielinski (Polish, b. 1948)
Manufacturer: raw material by Novamont S.p.A., Novara, Italy; manufacture of the cutlery by Cootrade, Unna, Germany
Date of design: 1995

Mater-Bi, a V-class material used to make rigid objects such as the examples here, is biodegradable, compostable, and soluble. The cutlery, while not notable for its design, is highly commendable for its ecologically minded features. Not currently available to the general consumer, these eating utensils were developed for McDonald's restaurants; more than 20 million pieces were produced in the first year. Other applications of Mater-Bi may also include any product now made from a slowly decomposing or non-degrading plastic, even drinking straws and dog bones.

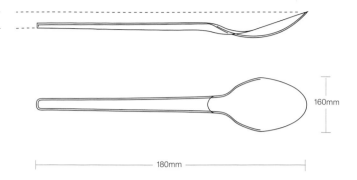

13mm

160mm

180mm

As an example of the flatware, only the dimensions of the spoon are listed here.

The production process begins with starch.

Starch and cellulose derivatives are formed into Mater-Bi pellets whose characteristics are comparable to those of polyolefins, a long-chain synthetic polymer.

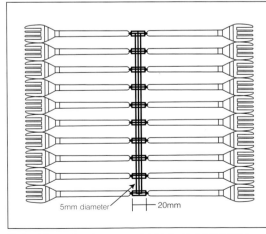

5mm diameter
20mm

Forks (shown here), spoons, and knives are injection molded in sets on a stem and then broken away.

A Test start	B After 10 days	C After 20 days	D After 30 days	E After 40 days
Mater-Bi samples	Weight loss 32,1%	Weight loss 55,7%	Weight loss 69%	Weight loss 90%

Mater-Bi Z101U/T composts within a very short time, losing 90% of its weight within 40 days.

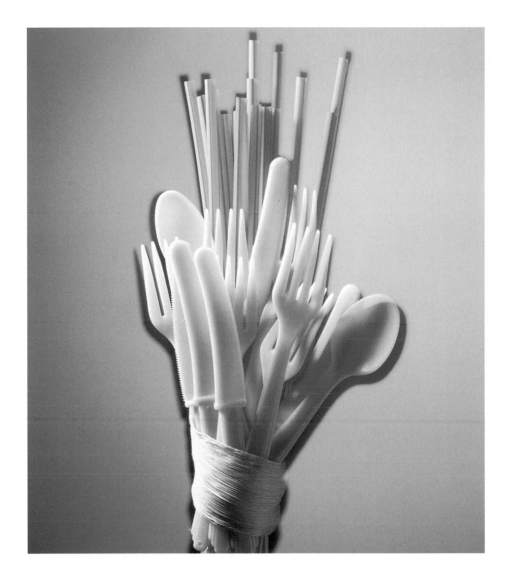

28

"Tiptap" bottle stopper

Designer: Joseph Ronen (Israeli, b. 1958)
Manufacturer: Progetti S.r.l., Carate Brianza
(MI), Italy
Date of design: 1995

This design solution is based on two principles
of chemistry: when a spoon, for example, is
inserted into the neck of a partially filled bottle,
the contents will remain unaltered, and, when an
air cushion is created on the surface of a liquid,
gas dispersion is prevented. This product, calling
on these two ideas, is evidence that intelligent
design may be more about problem solving
than mere aesthetics. About 10,000 pieces
have been produced at a price of 55,000 L.
($30, £18, 187 F.)

121mm
diameter

180mm

The stopper is made of die-cast solid 304 stainless steel,
either satin finished (left above) or polished (right above)

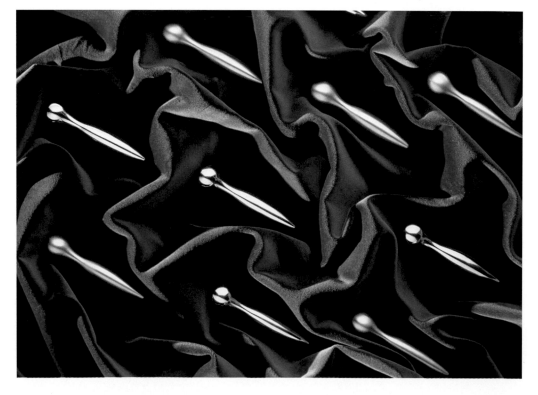

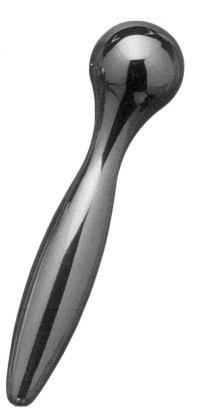

"Calmar à saumon" knife

Designers: Plan Créatif—Christophe Rebours
(French, b. 1966), project design manager
Manufacturer: Progexion, Rueil Malmaison, France
Date of design: 1997

A large industrial-design firm with offices worldwide was responsible for this domestic product.
However, the firm may be best known for more
ambitious assignments, such as those for vacuum
cleaners, telephones, and interiors. Not of interest
to everyone, this sleek streamline knife is used for
the preparation of an expensive food.

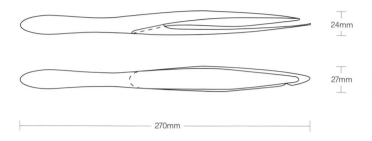

24mm

27mm

270mm

Available in stainless steel or ABS
(acrylonitrile-butadiene-styrene),

Cutting edges are honed along the bottom
side of the "mouth." The top edges are
not for cutting.

Each of the two sections are either welded (in
the steel version) or specially glued (in the
ABS version) at the backside of the "mouth."

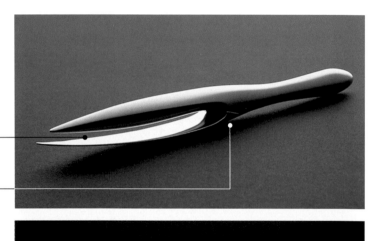

The top "jaw" of the "mouth" is somewhat
smaller than the cutting one on the bottom.

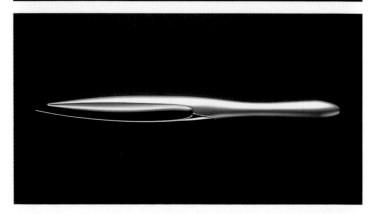

Dish

Designer: Alfred Kainz (German, b. 1960)
Manufacturer: the designer
Date of design: 1996

This unusual handmade vessel is produced by bonding layers of crystal, marble, and/or limestone with a special tinted glue. The strata are ground down until successive layers are revealed, lending the appearance of stone having been eroded by the forces of nature. Each piece is unique, and the designer considers them to be works of art.

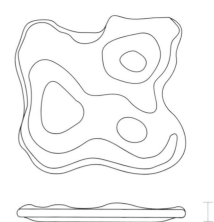

30mm

300mm

Because each example is handmade, sizes here are approximate.

The designer as craftsperson employs a hand-operated electrical diamond grinding wheel to wear away the layers of various natural materials.

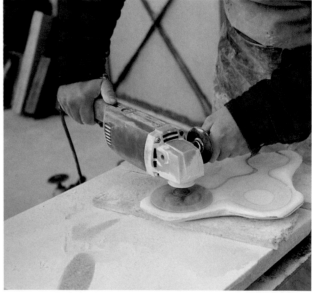

Notice that work is being done outside. The particles created by the grinding are airborne and harmful, necessitating a mask.

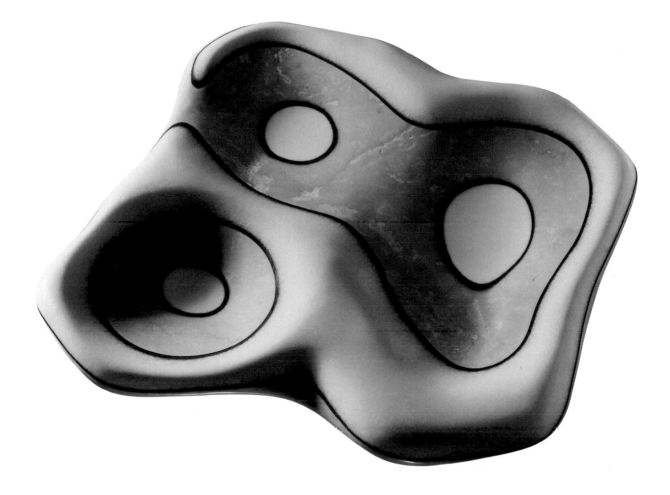

Dish

Epoxidharz (special epoxy glue) with color added bonds the layers of stone or crystal. Blue and brown were used in this example.

After grinding, polishing occurs. Each platter has individual characteristics of its own.

Personal Effects

"Wally" and "Spike" razors

Designer: Jack Hokanson (American, b. 1957)
Manufacturer: the designer's firm, Hoke2, Campbell, CA, U.S.A.

Interesting both for their use of an evanescent plastic material and for their practical function, these non-disposable razors offer a new twist to an old product. Two versions are available: the "Wally" with a suction cup as part of the base and the "Spike" with a separate suction cup from which the razor hangs.

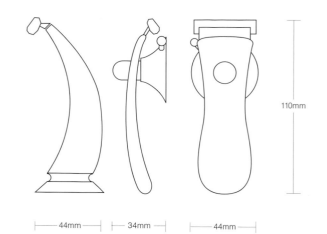

44mm   34mm   44mm   110mm

Non-slip handle.

Moveable suction-cup hanger.

Injection-molded transparent thermoplastic rubber.

Non-slip handle.

A suction cup is integrated into the base for adherence to smooth surfaces.

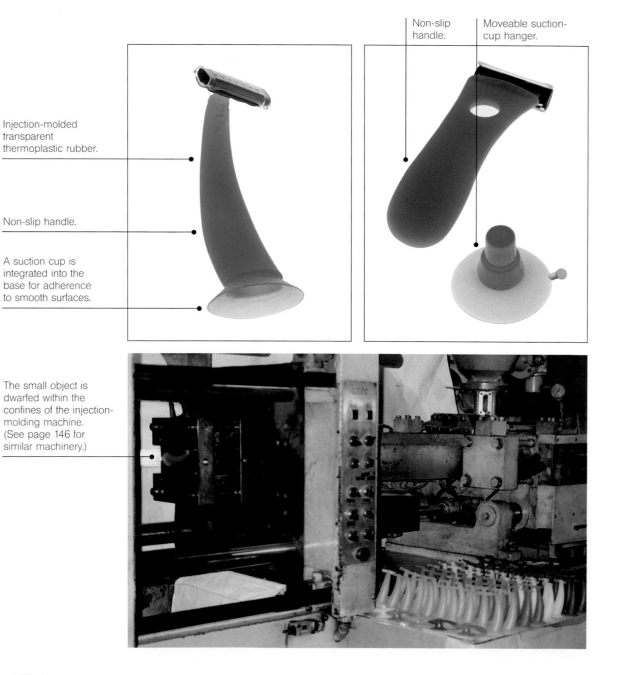

The small object is dwarfed within the confines of the injection-molding machine. (See page 146 for similar machinery.)

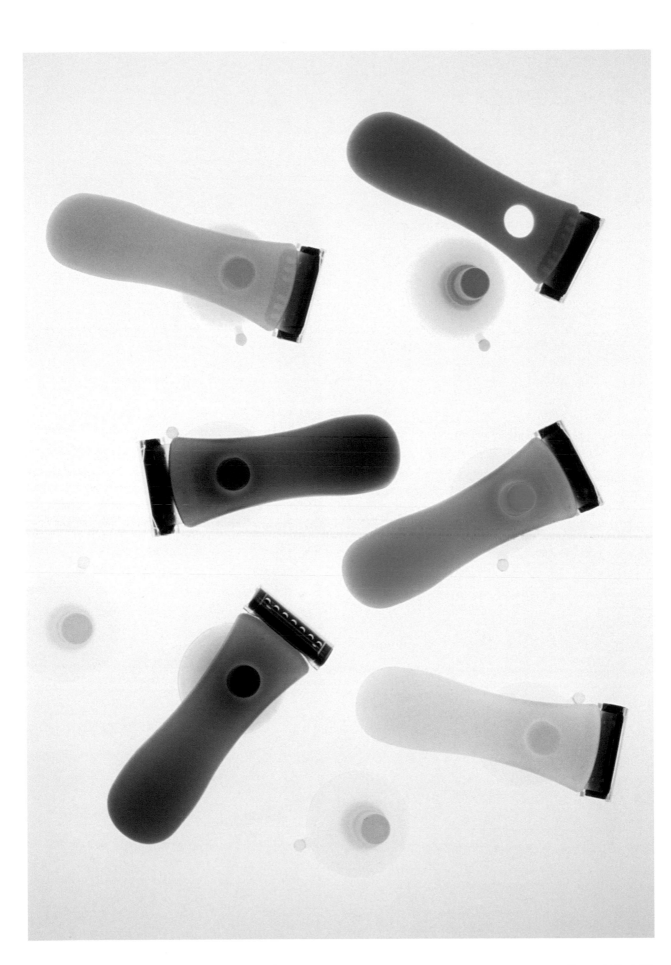

"Mr. Mause" clothes hanger

Designer: Sebastian Bergne (British, b. 1966)
Manufacturer: d-House, Fedra B.V., Lugano,
Switzerland
Date of design: 1996

The old technology for making bottle-cleaning
brushes is used in a unique manner here for
making clothes hangers. PVC bristles are wound
into a double zinc stem; thus, garments are given
a more filled-out shape than possible with thin
wire hangers. However, the expense ($34, £21,
202F. per hanger) could create the perception
that the product is more a novelty than a
necessary, highly functional utilitarian item.

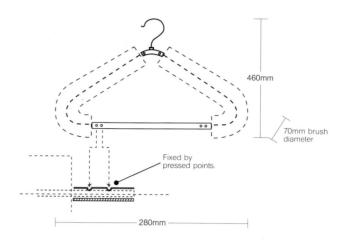

460mm

70mm brush
diameter

Fixed by
pressed points.

280mm

The bristle section is available in three colors or white.

Thin-wall
stainless-
steel tubing.

Solid stainless-
steel hook.

Rubber "O" ring.

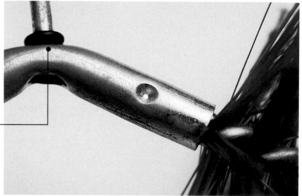

An automatic brush-
winding machine twists
two strands of soft wire
around PVC (poly-
vinylchloride) bristles.

"Bell" and "Pop Up" clothes hangers

Designers: Rossano Didaglio (Italian, b. 1956)
and Raimondo Sandri (Italian, b. 1966)
Manufacturer: Fly Line, Carré (VI), Italy
Date of design: 1997

This clothes-hanger design is available in two versions: the "Bell" shown on the facing page and the "Pop Up" shown below. According to the designers, they set out "to make an object that has always been kept hidden inside wardrobes aesthetically pleasant." Due to the colors and the inflated, puffy nature of the hanger, they also acknowledge that the object has a toy-like appearance.

880mm

510mm

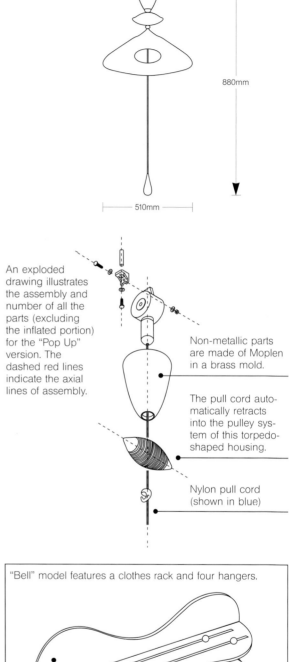

An exploded drawing illustrates the assembly and number of all the parts (excluding the inflated portion) for the "Pop Up" version. The dashed red lines indicate the axial lines of assembly.

Non-metallic parts are made of Moplen in a brass mold.

The pull cord automatically retracts into the pulley system of this torpedo-shaped housing.

Nylon pull cord (shown in blue)

"Pop Up" model attaches to the ceiling and is moveable up and down.

"Bell" model features a clothes rack and four hangers.

Lacquered aluminum rack.

Wardrobe box

Designer: Curro Claret Martin (Spanish, b. 1968)
Manufacturer: prototype
Date of design: 1996

This product began as a commission from
a young couple to solve a closet storage
problem. Initially, the designer himself made
about 20 examples for this client. The box
was later refined to feature a top which
occupied the full height in order to permit
expansion and provide a larger face on
which to announce the contents in chalk.

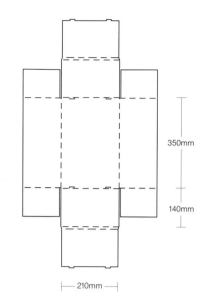

350mm

140mm

⊢— 210mm —⊣

Since the versions shown
here are small-production
models for a specific private
client, final mass production
specification would probably
be altered.

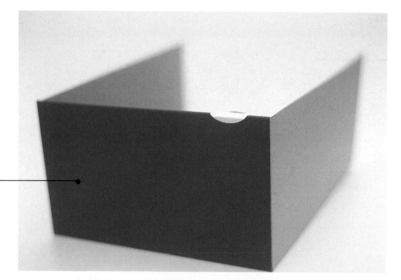

Slate paint on
corrugated cardboard.

Since chalk is used for marking
on the box faces, the designer
suggests its storage in a section
of the box itself.

34

Wardrobe box

As the printing on the faces indicates, slate paint and Aironfix were experiments.

A typical use of the wardrobe boxes, in the top section of a closet.

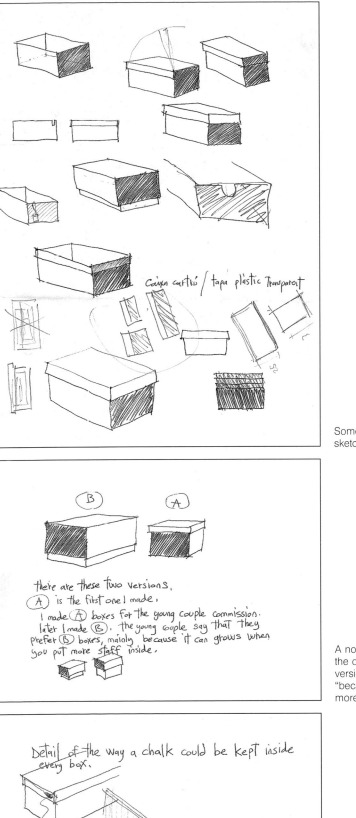

The sketch contains handwritten notes:

Caixa cartló / tapa plàstic Transparent

there are these two versions.
Ⓐ is the first one I made.
I made Ⓐ boxes for the young couple commission.
later I made Ⓑ. the young couple say that they
prefer Ⓑ boxes, mainly because it can grows when
you put more staff inside.

Detail of the way a chalk could be kept inside
every box.

chalk

Some of the designer's early
sketches.

A note on this drawing indicates that
the designer's clients preferred the
version at the top left (marked "B")
"because it grows when you put
more stuff inside," according to him.

As stated on the drawing, "Detail
of the way a [piece of] chalk could
be kept inside every box."

"Dune" clothes racks

Designers: Paolo Ulian (Italian, b. 1961) and
Giuseppe Ulian (Italian, b. 1959)
Manufacturer: Opposite S.n.c., Giorgio Sul
Legnano (MI), Italy
Date of design: 1996

If one were ignorant of the material employed
to make the pegs on these clothes racks,
the shrunken mineral-water bottles might
appear to be a valuable material—maybe
crystal or glass rather than merely
discarded plastic refuse. Since the bottle
mouths are already threaded, a specially
designed connector attached to the base
takes advantage of the feature.

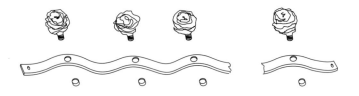

One peg: 200mm long x 80mm wide x 150mm high.
Three pegs: 750mm long x 80mm wide x 150mm high.
Six pegs: 1500mm long x 80mm wide x 150mm high.

The peg is a shrivelled PET
(polyethylene terephthalate)
mineral-water bottle, in azure,
yellow, or green.

The base structure is either
machine pressure-bent steel
(facing page) or heat printed
plastic (right).

The knobs are configured
in tandem with one, three,
or six pegs.

The bottle mouth is screwed
into, not onto, a special
receptacle attached to the
frame.

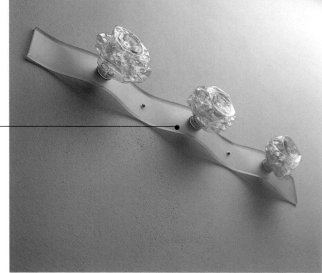

"Dune" clothes racks

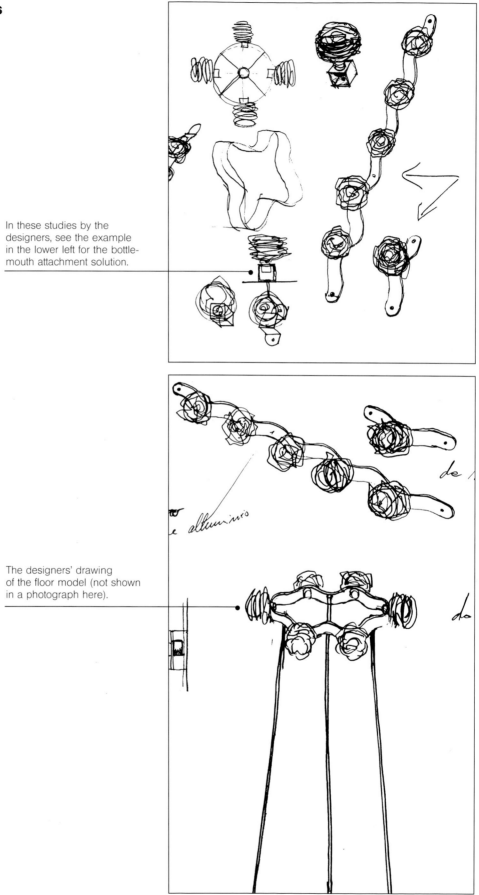

In these studies by the designers, see the example in the lower left for the bottle-mouth attachment solution.

The designers' drawing of the floor model (not shown in a photograph here).

Vases

"Amazing" vase

Designer: Johan Bakermans (Dutch,
b. 1971)
Manufacturer: Macek Technika B.V., Oss,
The Netherlands
Date of design: 1992

The designer conceived of this stackable and
unbreakable vase while an industrial-design
engineering student at the Polytechnic in The
Hague, and in 1997 production was begun
by the large manufacturer, Macek Technika.
During the first nine months of production,
150,000 pieces were made and sold at the
low retail price of 35 Dutch gulden ($20,
£12.50, 120F.).

140mm

330mm

160mm
diameter

Each of the two individual parts
is stackable.

The cone is injection-molded
SEBS (thermoplastic rubber)
in a Battenfeld BA 2000/1000
CDC (closing power 2000 kN)
single mold.

In the same material, the base is
injection molded in a Battenfeld
BA 950/500 CDC (closing power
950 kN) double mold.

The voluptuous malleability
of the cone section permits
infinite permutations.

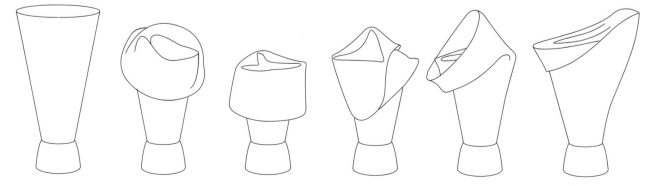

"Amazing" vase

The designer asserts that vases are usually designed without flowers which necessitates having to adjust the bouquet to the vase, rather than adjusting the vase to the bouquet. Yet another variation of the "Amazing" vase's accommodating malleability is shown here.

The designer's drawing (below) looks more like a photograph.

When the cones and bases are removed from the molds no finishing is needed due to the structure of the mold and the use of hot runners.

Vases being packed, stacked, and sorted (above and below). To reduce space in boxes and thereby trucks and shipping containers for transportation worldwide, the cones are stacked eight to a carton, and the bases are placed inside the cones.

"Bloemschikker" (wrinkle vase)

Designer: Martin Brühl (Dutch, b. 1954)
Manufacturer: the designer; distributed by
The Edge/Sample from Industry, Rotterdam,
The Netherlands
Date of design: 1996

This vessel is handmade by a designer who
has become known for his art furniture.
Produced from a single sheet of stainless
steel, the vase's similarity to Paolo Venini's
so-called handkerchief vase of the 1950s is
undeniable. However, the Venini vase was
produced with Murano glass melted over a
form rather than pressed, beaten, and bent
over a form, as in this metal version.

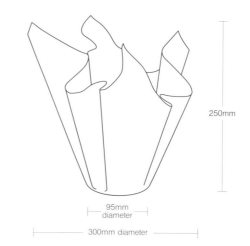

250mm

95mm
diameter

300mm diameter

Because each example is handmade, sizes are approximate.

First, a square piece of
stainless-steel sheeting is
bent using a lever press and
hammering over a form that
shapes the base. The white
coating is a foil that protects
the surface finish; it is removed
when the work is completed.

In the next stage, the sides are
formed by bending the folds
over a large wooden dowel.

A complete vase is shown
with the white foil removed.
Each example, due to its
hand-hewn nature, is different.

Inflated vase

Designers: Fernando Campana (Brazilian,
b. 1961) and Humberto Campana (Brazilian,
b. 1953.)
Manufacturer: Lidice Brinquedos Ltda.,
São Paulo, Brazil
Date of design: 1997

An array of large, powerful machines are
employed to realize what appears to be a
rather simple object. The translucency of
the PVC (polyvinylchloride) body imbues
the object with a fragile quality which is
counter to reality. Unlike inflated chairs for
example, this vase agreeably does not
gradually deflate during use; at least the
sample tested did not.

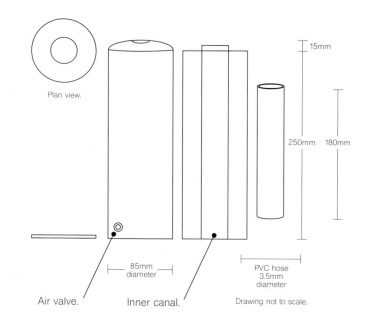

Plan view.

15mm

250mm   180mm

85mm
diameter

PVC hose
3.5mm
diameter

Air valve.   Inner canal.   Drawing not to scale.

Top section (PVC film) is heat
bonded to the body.

Body section (PVC film,
pneumatic grade,
.025mm thick).

Flexible tube (PVC, 2.5mm
diameter, 180 mm high)
serves as the inner canal that
holds the flower stem.

Sealable valve for inflation by
mouth blowing.

Compressed paper base
(85mm diameter, 4mm thick).

Inflated vase

A worker slits PVC film with electric shears to workable, non-specific dimensions.

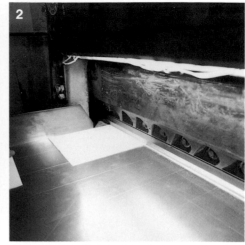

A pneumatic guillotine press, like a paper cutter, shears the inner and outer sections of the cylinder.

A worker at a pneumatic press stamps out the bottom disk, using a die, from corrugated cardboard.

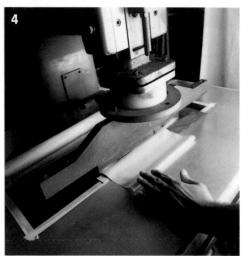

The cylinder film is rolled and joined by heat welding.

The cylinder, after welding into an envelope, is turned inside out, and the inflation value is heat welded in place.

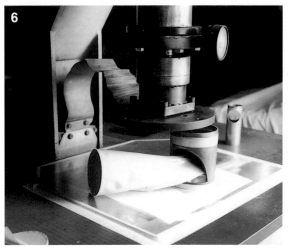

The four major components (outer cylinder, inner cylinder, top and bottom disks) are heat welded together; here the inner cylinder is fused to the top and bottom disks.

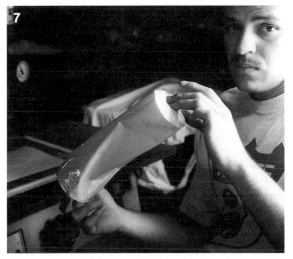

A worker holds a fully assembled vase before the inner tube is put in place.

During the final stage of assembly, a worker inserts the clear PVC tube that will eventually hold water and glues it in place.

39

"Travel Vase"

Designers: Gabriella Dorligo (Italian, b. 1962) and
Maurizio Martinelli (Italian, b. 1959)
Manufacturer: the designers
Date of design: 1996

The design of this unorthodox object is based
on the premise that a vase can be lightweight
but strong while being dismountable for
storage when not in use. As a play on the vase
metaphor, the bag itself suggests a flower shape.
Even though the designers suggest that this vase
may be taken along on trips, this function may
not be a niche people want filled.

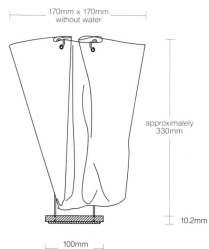

170mm x 170mm
without water

approximately
330mm

10.2mm

100mm
x 100mm

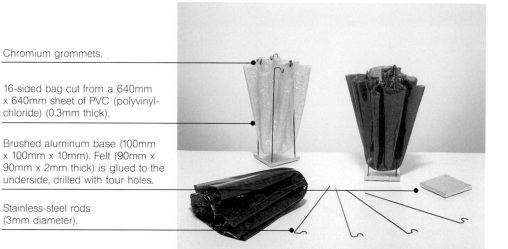

Chromium grommets.

16-sided bag cut from a 640mm
x 640mm sheet of PVC (polyvinylchloride) (0.3mm thick).

Brushed aluminum base (100mm
x 100mm x 10mm). Felt (90mm x
90mm x 2mm thick) is glued to the
underside, drilled with four holes.

Stainless-steel rods
(3mm diameter).

40

"A Vase"

Designer: Anish Kapoor (Indian, b. 1954)
Manufacturer: Slegten & Toegemann S.A.,
Brussels, Belgium
Date of design: 1992

For a vase, this designer-sculptor calls upon
the sexually evocative themes frequently found
in his fine art. The three sections of this work
representing the male form, the female form,
and the earth are intended to be placed in
either of two positions. This piece, in an edition
of 900, was produced in collaboration with
industrial designer Torsten Fritze.

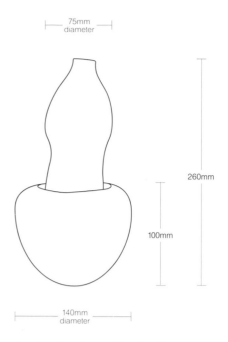

75mm
diameter

260mm

100mm

140mm
diameter

Vase elements are in an upright position. The
terracotta element (not shown above) measures
70mm high × 150mm wide × 100mm deep.

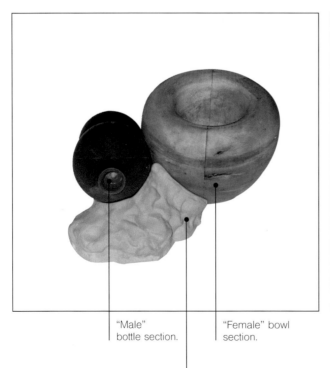

"Male"
bottle section.

"Female" bowl
section.

"Earth" form.

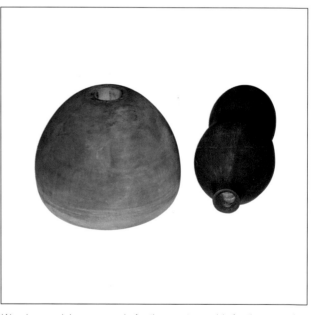

Wooden models were made for the master molds for the ceramic,
glass, or terracotta casting. Versions are produced in ceramic or
frosted mouth-blown glass for the "male" and "female" sections
and terracotta for the "earth" section.

41

"Sponge vase"

Designer: Marcel Wanders (Dutch, b. 1963)
Manufacturer: prototype by Wanders Wonders, Amsterdam, The Netherlands; produced from mid-1998 as a joint project by Droog Design, Amsterdam, and Rosenthal AG, Selb, Germany
Date of design: 1997

It would not be possible to achieve the fine, thin character of porcelain that real substances can produce. For example, this vase was made by saturating a sponge with liquefied clay and firing it in a standard ceramic kiln. The sponge burns away leaving a delicate ghost of itself behind.

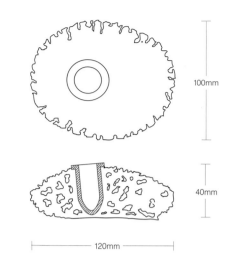

100mm

40mm

120mm

Because the dimensions and shape of each sponge varies greatly, sizes here are approximate.

The well for flowers is molded in clay and inserted into the sponge before firing.

After firing, the slip-saturated sponge completely disappears, and only a copy remains.

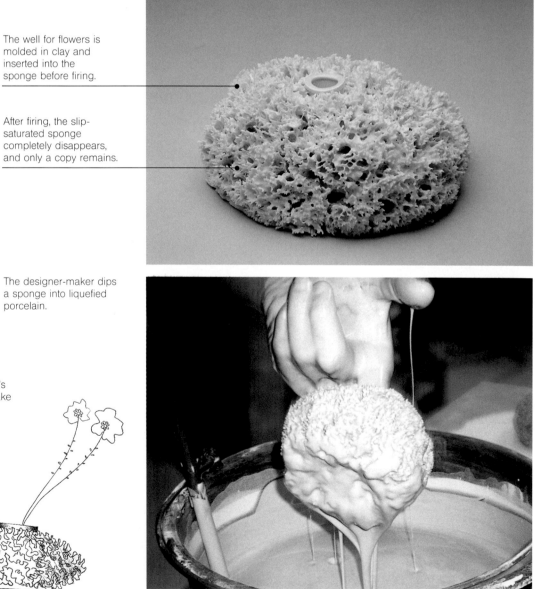

The designer-maker dips a sponge into liquefied porcelain.

One of the designer's drawings should make it clear that every sponge is different in shape.

"Sponge vase"

Sponges on a table are ready for processing.

A sponge is dipped into slip (liquefied clay).

Above and middle right, excess slip is drained off.

The designer-maker uses his finger to make an opening for the tubular receptacle.

A tubular receptacle, made of
clay, is removed from a mold.

In an experiment, an exaggerated
porcelain receptacle into which
flowers are to be inserted
protrudes from a fired sponge.

"Autoritratto in forma di vaso"
(self-portrait in the shape of a vase)

Designer: Gaetano Pesce (Italian, b. 1939)
Manufacturer: the designer
Date of design: 1997–98

The furniture, furnishings, and lighting of this prolific
designer, known for his innovative work in plastics,
are normally produced in multiples. However,
they are frequently unique due to the nature of the
manufacturing process, unpredictable manipulation
of plastics, and the designer's methodology. This
piece is exceptional in that it is one of a kind and
expensive at $40,000 (£24,000, 225,000 F.).

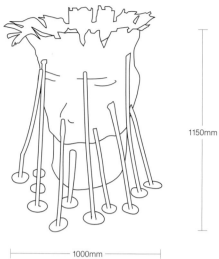

1150mm

1000mm

Even though the main body of
this vase is produced by casting
polyurethane resin in a mold,
polyurethane rods, serving as
legs, are attached for support.
"Feet" are formed by the resin
coating that has puddled.

The wall thickness (4–5mm)
is built up by successive
coatings of polyurethane
resin.

42

"Autoritratto in forma di vaso"
(self-portrait in the shape of a vase)

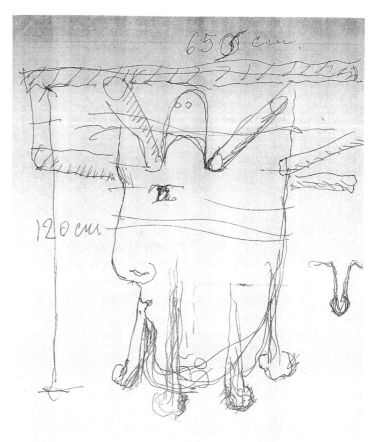

The face in the designer-maker's drawings attests to the claim of self-portraiture.

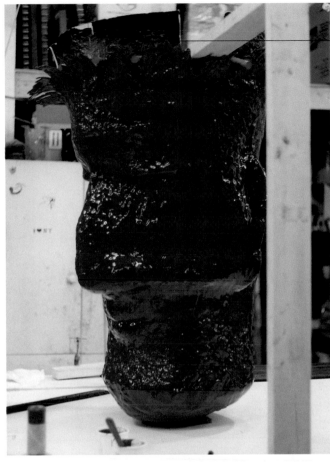

The mold before its removal and before support rods are added.

The designer-maker brush paints the support rods with polyurethane.

43

"Vase d'avril"

Designers: Tsé & Tsé Associées—Catherine
Lévy and Sigolène Prébois (both French,
b. 1964)
Manufacturer: the designers' firm, Tsé &
Tsé Associées, Paris, France
Date of design: 1991

This vase is composed of 21 glass tubes,
similar to those used by chemists, that are
inserted into 20 interlocking metal fixtures.
The shape can be arranged in a diverse
number of positions. When one of the
tubes is removed, the tail ends of the fixture can be joined to create a ring. Also,
the length can be shorted by removing
tubes. When purchased, an extra tube is
included in case of breakage.

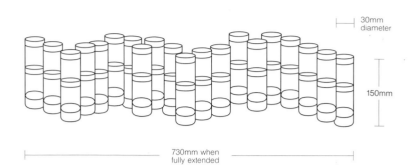

30mm
diameter

150mm

730mm when
fully extended

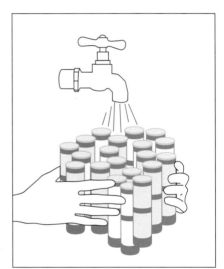

Illustrations adapted from drawings provided by the designers.

A glass tube acts like, for
example, the stem in a
hinge, and, when removed,
the unit becomes separated
into individual units.

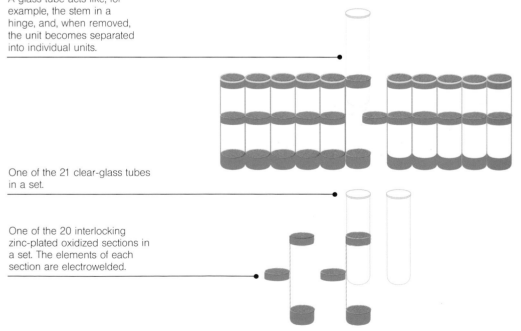

One of the 21 clear-glass tubes
in a set.

One of the 20 interlocking
zinc-plated oxidized sections in
a set. The elements of each
section are electrowelded.

44

"Vase of Dead Trees" (Fossil Series)

Designer: Makoto Komatsu (Japanese, b. 1943)
Manufacturer: the designer's firm,
product M, Saitama, Japan
Date of design: 1991

Based on the Japanese folk tale about an old man who magically could encourage dead trees to produce blossoms, this vase features a base (representing the earth) in a synthetic material that may be fully or partially filled with miniature vases (representing trees). Even though the designer claims that the examples shown here are prototypes, obviously a great deal of effort went into their production.

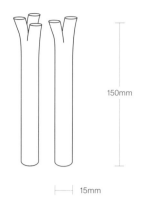

150mm

15mm

As configured here, a base may be partially filled with miniature vases.

Ceramic "trees" serve as vases.

The base (500mm x 500mm) is a polycarbonate material made to appear like glass.

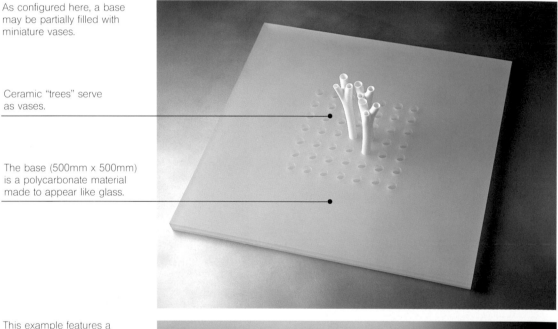

This example features a variation on the base treatment.

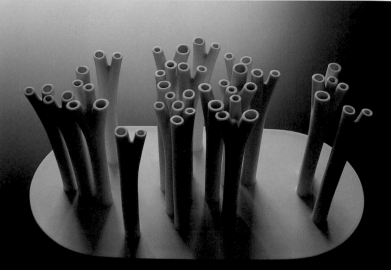

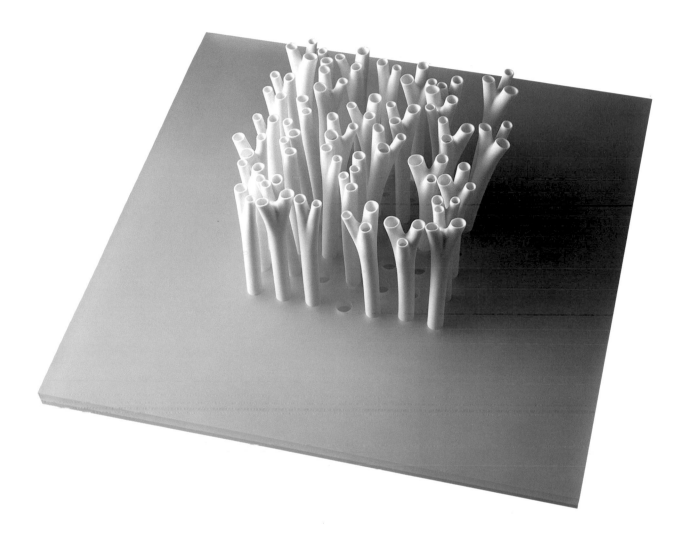

**"Vase of Dead Trees"
(Fossil Series)**

Closed and bound two- and three-part molds for two- and three-limb "trees" are ready for slip (liquefied ceramic material) to be poured.

Slip is being poured into a two-limb mold.

Excess slip is being poured out so that the "tree" limbs will be formed hollow.

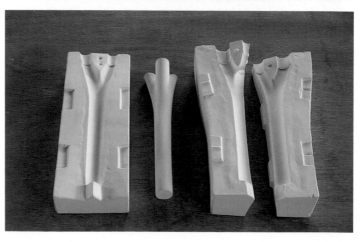

A three-limb "tree" is removed after being formed in a three-part mold. A three-part mold is necessary due to the three-dimensional nature of the limb. (For the same problem see pp. 66–69.)

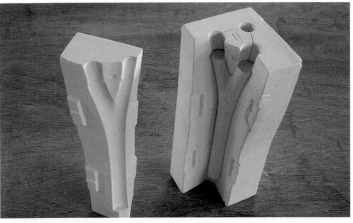

A closer view of two parts of a three-part mold.

The two different individual vases, or "trees," into which flower stems are eventually inserted when in use.

After molding, unglazed stems are reduction fired in a kiln and finished off with sandpaper.

45

"Erbale" plant holder

Designers: Fabio Bortolani (Italian, b. 1957),
Walter Becchelli (Italian, b. 1963), and
Stefano Maffei (Italian, b. 1966)
Manufacturer: d-House, Fedra B.V., Lugano,
Switzerland
Date of design: 1995

Employing heat-sealable, clear-plastic sheeting,
this plant holder is suspended from a rod and
can also serve as a room divider. It accommo-
dates both plants and water—the latter provided
by intravenous-like drip vessels like those used
in hospitals. Even though this product may not
prove to be long lasting and is probably difficult
to clean, it is nevertheless imaginative and
provocative.

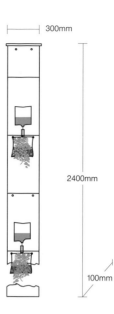

300mm

2400mm

100mm

Wash drawings by one
of the designers.

Each hanging flat sheet (2400mm x 300mm) includes
four bags for plants and four bags for water—all in
clear PVC (polyvinylchloride) (0.3mm).

There are four water-
and-plant units in each
vertical section.

Small galvanized steel
chain (no hooks).

Metal snaps attach
the bag.

Water.

Through a nozzle, water
drips into soil in the
bag below.

Beechwood stick is
heat-sealed in the seam.

Metal snaps attach
the bag.

Soil.

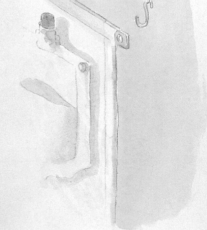

"Flowerjar"

Designer: Arnout Visser (Dutch, b. 1961)
Manufacturer: The Edge/Sample from
Industry, Rotterdam, The Netherlands
Date of design: 1994

The original materials from which this vase
is made are so appreciably altered that they
are unrecognizable. Offered with an etched
body, this vessel is made in two parts: a
glass mineral-water bottle of a specific brand
and a concrete-and-glass base. One version
features a clear dot pattern around the rim.

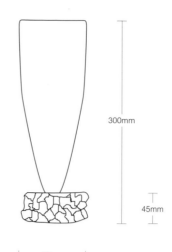

300mm

45mm

85mm

Only Sourcy mineral-water bottles are used to make this product. The brand name
and the bottle shape are registered by the Dutch distributor, Vrumona B.V., in Bunnik.

A bottle
with the bottom
removed.

Dry concrete to which
a black pigment is
added before molding.

A molded,
partially
treated base.

Ground tempered
glass (like in cars)
is used in the base.

"Flowerjar"

Sandblasting (with a course grain) a plastic mineral water bottle.

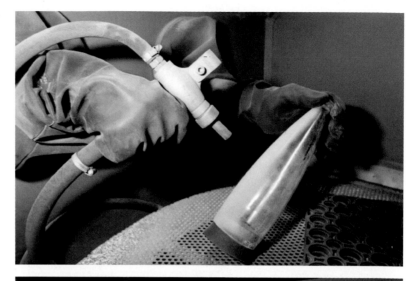

A mixture of ground glass, concrete, black pigment, and water for the base.

Exploded glass that occurs from destroyed B-quality tempered panes.

A grey PVC ring (split for easy removal) is set into a yellow plastic saucer and filled with the mixture used to make the base.

Concrete and a black pigment.

The concrete-and-glass base is sandblasted after being formed to create a very rough surface.

A special epoxy glue adheres the mouth of an inverted glass mineral-water bottle to the base. The glue also prevents water leakage.

Waste Bins

"Joker" waste bin

Designers: Sebastian Bergne (British,
b. 1966) and Stefanie Kubanek (German,
b. 1976)
Manufacturer: prototype for Zeus Etno Locic
exhibition, 1997; production version in
development
Date of design: 1997

Like certain versions of a top hat (in its
pop-up nature) or a tent for camping (in its
use of materials), this waste bin bursts into
full shape when released from its packing.
The highly flexible nature of fiberglass
rods permits collapsing into a flat shape,
a feature that helps to lessen shipping
and packing costs. The designers worked
directly on prototypes, eliminating a
conceptual-sketch or drawing stage.

Closed:
405mm diameter
x 10mm high

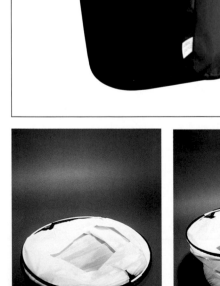

Fiberglass-rod frame.

Rip-stop nylon sewn
by semi-automatic
machines.

Opened:
405mm diameter
x 405mm high

Assembly by hand;
no glue was used.

The pop-up feature of this waste bin is demonstrated by
the first prototype below.

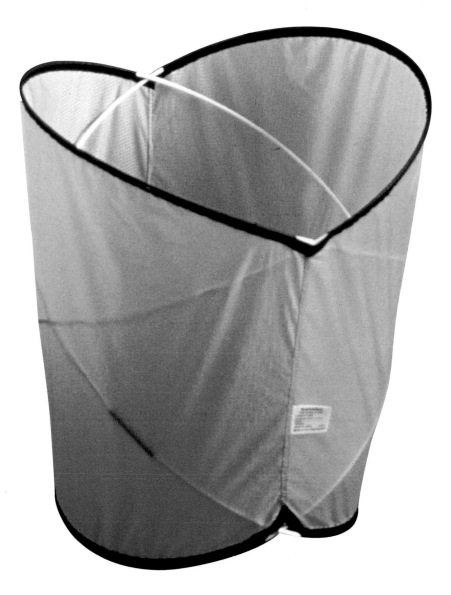

"Aero Bin"

Designer: Winfried Scheuer (German, b. 1952)
Manufacturer: Aero, London, Great Britain
Date of design: 1994

Since the three flat pieces that make up this product are essentially unimpressive until the user assembles them, the packaging becomes an important selling tool. With amusing messages and information about recycling and ecological issues printed on the package, the product is made more appealing.

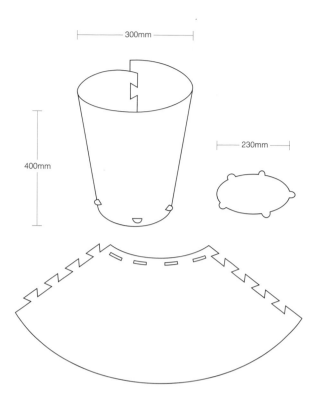

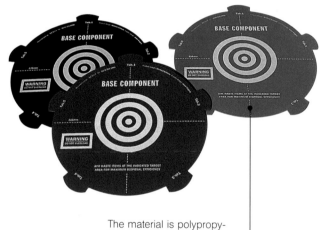

The material is polypropylene sheeting. The bottom (above) is silkscreened in two colors, and the sides (right) remain plain.

No glue or tools are required for assembly. Instructions are provided on the front of the packaging.

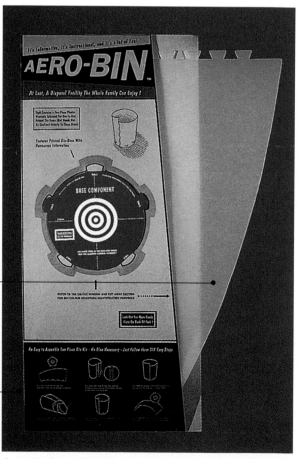

A metal-edge cutting die, inset into a wooden base, is used to stamp out both parts. This is the same inexpensive method employed for cardboard-box manufacture.

"De Paperbag" waste bin

Designer: Jos van der Meulen (Dutch, b. 1958)
Manufacturer: Goods, Amsterdam, The
Netherlands
Date of design: 1995

This waste bin is made of unused billboard
posters that feature larger-than-life images in
exaggerated halftone patterns and bold letters.
With sections sewn together, the end user pur-
chases the bag flat and molds it into
shape. Rigid neatness is not necessary for
the best results.

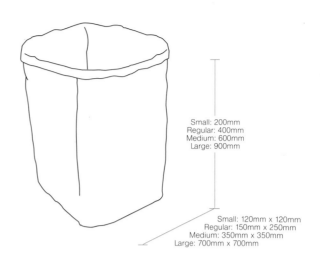

Small: 200mm
Regular: 400mm
Medium: 600mm
Large: 900mm

Small: 120mm x 120mm
Regular: 150mm x 250mm
Medium: 350mm x 350mm
Large: 700mm x 700mm

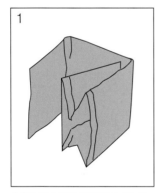

1

A flat bag with machine-sewn
seams.

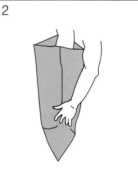

2

The bag is opened and
shaping begins.

3

The top edges are turned to
make a rim.

4

The rim is rolled over firmly.

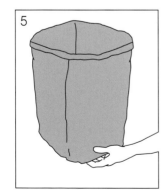

5

The bottom is pushed flat
and made square.

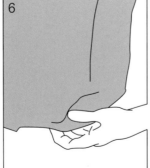

6

The corners are pushed out
from the inside.

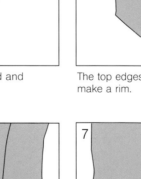

7

The bottom edges are flattened
from the inside out.

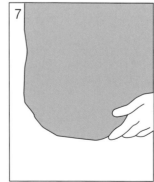

8

The full shape is straightened
out and modeled.

"Eco" waste bin

Designer: Raul Barbieri (Italian, b. 1946)
Manufacturer: Rexite S.p.A., Cusago
(MI), Italy
Date of design: 1993

As the designer has declared, his goal here
was to create a clean, minimal object with a
strong personality that would appeal to the
masses. The inventory is available in two
materials: opaque ABS (acrylonitrile-butadiene-styrene) and translucent polypropylene.
The polished inside wall of each bin is easy
to clean, and the rough outside skin resists
soiling. Of course, the main feature of this
somewhat inexpensive product is the rim
ring that covers the top edges of a standard
plastic-film waste-bag liner and holds it firm.

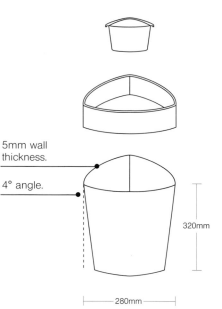

5mm wall thickness.

4° angle.

320mm

280mm

Available in ABS
(acrylonitrile-butadiene-
styrene) (below) as
well as polypropylene.

The so-called ecological
tub is used to separate
certain items from the
rest of the waste.

Plastic-film inner bag
is held in place by
the rim ring (in red
below).

"Ecological tub."

Plastic-bag ring holder.

Waste bin.

"Eco" waste bin

The range in translucent polypropylene.

A waste bin has been formed under high heat and 500 tons of pressure. The same worm channels are used for both ABS or polypropylene injections.

The oleodynamic press is regulated by a microprocessor.

The male die (shown below) is polished; the female die (outside of the bin and not shown) is textured by photoengraving.

A worker is removing a fully formed bin.

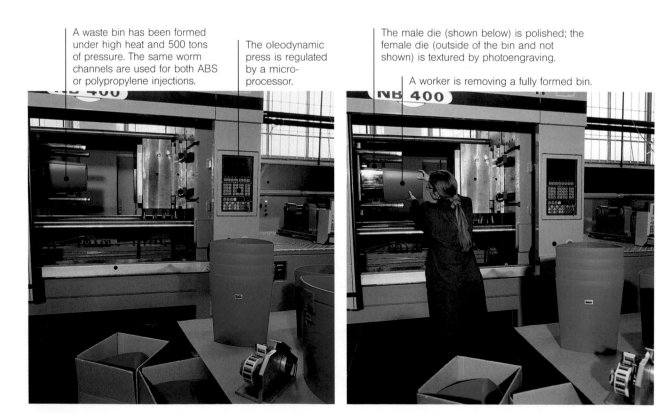

The range in opaque ABS
(acrylonitrile-butadiene-styrene).

Designers and Manufacturers

Designers

Manufacturers (if not by designers)

Acknowledgements and Permissions

Acknowledgments

The ProDesign series was developed from an original idea by the late Jean Koefoed.

Mel Byars, Cinzia Anguissola d'Altoé, and Brice d'Antras are very appreciative of the assistance and, due to our abnormal requests for process documentation, the patience we received from designers, manufacturers, colleagues, and friends in the preparation of this book.

Permissions

Photography was generously provided by the following contributors, preceded by page numbers:

12–13 Pieter van der Meer and WACC's Design & Consultancy
14 courtesy spOre
15 Jim Linna
16 courtesy Bruno Gregori
17 We Shoot
18–19 courtesy Alessi S.p.A.
20–21 courtesy Jeffrey Bernett
22–23 courtesy Massimo Varetto and Opos
24 (top row) Herr Kern, Krebs Glas Lauscha GmbH
24 (bottom row)–25 Kai Georg
26–27 Olivier Peyricot
28–32 Radi
34–37 Carlo Bevlacqua
38 (bottom)–39 Twan de Veer
40–41 courtesy Takahiro Okamoto and Eyetopia
42–43 courtesy Bernard Moïsc
44 (top)–45 Twan de Veer
44 (bottom row) courtesy The Edge/ Sample from Industry
46–48 Marcel Moermans
50–51 Olimpia Lalli
52 courtesy Sỳn
54–55 Billy Leung
56 (bottom left)–57 Chris Frazer Smith
56 (top left) Wanted S.n.c. di Francesco Bellesia
56 (top right, bottom left) courtesy Julian Brown
58 (top) courtesy Inflate Ltd
58 (bottom)–59 Jason Tozer
60–61 courtesy Jean-Marie Massaud and Authentics of antipresent GmbH
62–65 courtesy tranSglass
66–67 Ole Akhøj
68 (top) drawing by Ole Jensen
68 (bottom)–69 Per Folkver
72–75 Christopher Allen Procter
76–77 Santi Caveca
78–79 Ross Menuez
80–81 courtesy Novamont S.p.A.
82–83 Carlo Peffiarino and Massimo Montagnoli
84–85 courtesy Plan Créatif
86 courtesy Alfred Kainz
87–88 Foto Design Herbert Stolz
90–91 courtesy Hoke2
92–93 Emilio Tremolada
94–95 Lorenzo Cattelan
96–98 Rafael Vargas
100–101 Paolo Ulian

104–107 courtesy Bakermans Produktideeén
108 courtesy The Edge/Sample from Industry
109 Herman van Adrichem
110–113 Andrés Otero
114 Tiziano Neppi
116–117 courtesy Slegten & Toegemann
118 (top) Hans van der Mars
118 (bottom), 120–121 courtesy Marcel Wanders
119 Jonathan Xena
122–125 courtesy Pesce Ltd.
126 127 Kleinnefen
128–131 Fujitsuka Mitsumasa
132–133 Tom Vack
134, 136 courtesy The Edge/Sample from Industry
135 Twan de Veer
138–139 Sebastian Bergne
140–141 courtesy Winfried Scheuer and Aero
143 Sigurd Kranendonk
144–147 Mario Tedeschi

General Index

General Index